BARON D'HOLBACH

A STUDY OF EIGHTEENTH CENTURY RADICALISM IN FRANCE

BY

MAX PEARSON CUSHING

SUBMITTED IN PARTIAL FULFILMENT OF THE REQUIREMENTS FOR THE DEGREE OF DOCTOR OF PHILOSOPHY, IN THE FACULTY OF POLITICAL SCIENCE, COLUMBIA UNIVERSITY

NEW YORK
1914

Cover adapted from *Paul Heinrich Dietrich Baron d'Holbach*, 1785, by Alexander Roslin

ISBN: 978-1-78139-112-9

Printed on acid free ANSI archival quality paper.

Table of Contents

BARON D'HOLBACH

A une extréme justesse d'esprit il joignait une simplicité de moeurs tout-à-fait antique et patriarcale.[1]

J. A. NAIGEON, *Journal de Paris*, le 9 fev. 1789

[1] [The current editor has added translations of the French (and, in one case, German) quotations throughout the text, these additions are denoted by footnotes in square brackets:

"To extreme mental acuity he added a simplicity of manners that was both old-fashioned and patriarchal."]

INTRODUCTION

Diderot, writing to the Princess Dashkoff in 1771, thus analysed the spirit of his century:

Chaque siècle a son esprit qui le caractérise. L'esprit du nôtre semble être celui de la liberté. La première attaque contre la superstition a été violente, sans mesure. Une fois que les hommes ont osé d'une manière quelconque donner l'assaut à la barrière de la religion, cette barrière la plus formidable qui existe comme la plus respectée, il est impossible de s'arrêter. Dès qu'ils ont tourné des regards menaçants contre la majesté du ciel, ils ne manqueront pas le moment d'après de les diriger contre la souveraineté de la terre. Le câble qui tient et comprime l'humanité est formé de deux cordes, l'une ne peut céder sans que l'autre vienne à rompre.[1]

The following study proposes to deal with this attack on religion that preceded and helped to prepare the French Revolution. Similar phenomena are by no means rare in the annals of history; eighteenth-century atheism, however, is of especial interest, standing as it does at the end of a long period

---

[1] Diderot, *Oeuvres*, ed. Assézat et Tourneaux, Vol. XX, p. 28.

[Every century has a characteristic spirit. The spirit of ours seems to be that of freedom. The first attack against superstition was violent beyond measure. Once men have dared in some way to storm the gate of religion, the most formidable barrier that exists because it is the most respected, it is impossible to stop. Having turned menacing looks against the majesty of heaven, they will not pass up the opportunity to turn against earthly sovereignty. The cable that holds and compresses humanity consists of two strands, one cannot give way without leading to the other breaking.]

of theological and ecclesiastical disintegration and prophesying a reconstruction of society on a purely rational and naturalistic basis. The anti-theistic movement has been so obscured by the less thoroughgoing tendency of deism and by subsequent romanticism that the real issue in the eighteenth century has been largely lost from view. Hence it has seemed fit to center this study about the man who stated the situation with the most unmistakable and uncompromising clearness, and who still occupies a unique though obscure position in the history of thought.

Holbach has been very much neglected by writers on the eighteenth century. He has no biographer. M. Walferdin wrote (in an edition of Diderot's Works, Paris, 1821, Vol. XII p. 115): "Nous nous occupons depuis longtemps à rassembler les matériaux qui doivent servir à venger la mémoire du philosophe de la patrie de Leibnitz, et dans l'ouvrage que nous nous proposons de publier sous le titre "D'Holbach jugé par ses contemporains" nous espérons faire justement apprécier ce savant si estimable par la profondeur et la variété de ses connaissances, si précieux à sa famille et à ses amis par la pureté et la simplicité de ses mœurs, en qui la vertu était devenue une habitude et la bienfaisance un besoin." This work has never appeared and M. Tourneux thinks that nothing of it was found among M. Walferdin's papers.[2] In 1834 Mr. James Watson published in an English translation of the *Système de la Nature*, *A Short Sketch of the Life and the Writings of Baron d'Holbach* by Mr. Julian Hibbert, compiled especially for that edition from Saint Saurin's article in Michaud's *Biographie Universelle* (Paris, 1817, Vol. XX, pp. 460-467), from Barbier's *Dict. des ouvrages anonymes* (Paris, 1822) and from the preface to the Paris edition of the *Système de la Nature* (4 vols., 18mo, 1821). This sketch was later published separately (London, 1834, 12mo, pp. 14) but on account of the author's sudden death it was left

[2] Grimm, *Corr. Lit.*, Vol. XV, p. 421.

unfinished and is of no value from the point of view of scholarship. Another attempt to publish something on Holbach was made by Dr. Anthony C. Middleton of Boston in 1857. In the preface to his translation to the *Lettres à Eugenia* he speaks of a "Biographical Memoir of Baron d'Holbach which I am now preparing for the press." If ever published at all this *Memoir* probably came to light in the *Boston Investigator*, a free-thinking magazine published by Josiah P. Mendum, 45 Cornhill, Boston, but it is not to be found. Mention should also be made of the fact that M. Assézat intended to include in a proposed study of Diderot and the philosophical movement, a chapter to be devoted to Holbach and his society; but this work has never appeared.[3]

Of the two works bearing Holbach's name as a title, one is a piece of libellous fiction by Mme. de Genlis, *Les Diners du baron d'Holbach* (Paris, 1822, 8vo), the other a romance pure and simple by F. T. Claudon (Paris, 1835, 2 vols., 8vo) called *Le Baron d'Holbach*, the events of which take place largely at his house and in which he plays the rôle of a minor character. A good account of Holbach, though short and incidental, is to be found in M. Avézac-Lavigne's *Diderot et la Société du Baron d'Holbach* (Paris, 1875, 8vo), and M. Armand Gasté has a little book entitled *Diderot et le cure de Montchauvet, une Mystification littéraire chez le Baron d'Holbach* (Paris, 1895, 16vo). There are several works which devote a chapter or section to Holbach.[4] The French critics and the histories of philosophy

---

[3] Diderot, *Oeuvres*, Vol. XX, p. 95.

[4] Among the most important are Damiron J. P., *Mémoires pourservir à l'histoire de la philosophie au dix-huitième siècle* (Paris, 1858, 3 vols., 8vo); Lange, *Geschichte des Materialismus* (Eng. tr., Boston, 1877); Morley, *Diderot and the Encyclopedists* (N. Y., 1891, 2 vols., 12mo); Plekhanow, G., *Beiträge zur Geschichte des Materialismus* (Stuttgart, 1896); Hancock, A. E., *The French Revolution and the English Poets* (N. Y., 1899); Tallentyre, *The Friends of Voltaire* (London, 1906); Fabre, *Les Pères de la Révolution* (Paris, 1910), etc.

contain slight notices; Rosenkranz's "Diderot's Leben" devotes a chapter to Granval, Holbach's country seat, and life there as described by Diderot in his letters to Mlle. Volland; and he is included in such histories of ideas as Soury, J., "Bréviaire de l'histoire de Matérialisme" (Paris, 1881) and Delvaille, J., *Essai sur l'histoire de l'idée de progrès* (Paris, 1910); but nowhere else is there anything more than the merest encyclopedic account, often defective and incorrect.

The sources are in a sense full and reliable for certain phases of his life and literary activity. His own publications, numbering about fifty, form the most important body of source material for the history and development of his ideas. Next in importance are contemporary memoirs and letters including those of Voltaire, Rousseau, Diderot, Grimm, Morellet, Marmontel, Mme. d'Epinay, Naigeon, Garat, Galiani, Hume, Garrick, Wilkes, Romilly and others; and scattered letters by Holbach himself, largely to his English friends. In addition there is a large body of contemporary hostile criticism of his books, by Voltaire, Frederick II, Castillon, Holland, La Harpe, Delisle de Sales and a host of outraged ecclesiastics, so that one is well informed in regard to the scandal that his books caused at the time. Out of these materials and other scattered documents and notices it is possible to reconstruct—though somewhat defectively—the figure of a man who played an important rôle in his own day; but whose name has long since lost its significance—even in the ears of scholars. It is at the suggestion of Professor James Harvey Robinson that this reconstruction has been made. If it shall prove of any interest or value he must be credited with the initiation of the idea as well as constant aid in its realization. For rendering possible the necessary investigations, recognition is due to the administration and officers of the Bibliothèque Nationale, the British Museum, the Library of Congress, the Libraries of Columbia and Harvard Universities, Union and Andover Theological Seminaries, and the Public Libraries of Boston and New York.

M. P. C.—NEW YORK CITY,—July, 1914.

Chapter I.
Holbach, the Man.

Paul Heinrich Dietrich, or as he is better known, Paul-Henri Thiry, baron d'Holbach, was born in January, 1723, in the little village of Heidelsheim (N.W. of Carlsruhe) in the Palatinate. Of his parentage and youth nothing is known except that his father, a rich parvenu, according to Rousseau,[1] brought him to Paris at the age of twelve, where he received the greater part of his education. His father died when Holbach was still a young man. It may be doubted if young Holbach inherited his title and estates immediately as there was an uncle "Messire Francois-Adam, Baron d'Holbach, Seigneur de Héeze, Léende et autres Lieux" who lived in the rue Neuve S. Augustin and died in 1753. His funeral was held at Saint-Roch, his parish church, Thursday, September 16th, where he was afterward entombed.[2] Holbach was a student in the University of Leyden in 1746 and spent a good deal of time at his uncle's estate at Héeze, a little town in the province of North Brabant (S.E. of Eindhoven). He also traveled and studied in Germany. There are two manuscript letters in the British Museum (Folio 30867, pp. 14, 18, 20) addressed by Holbach to John Wilkes, which throw some light on his school-days. It is interesting to note that most of Holbach's friends were young Englishmen of whom there were

---

[1] Confessions, *Oeuvres*, Vol. XXIV, p. 338.

[2] Bib. Nat. mss. *Pièces originales,* 1529, d'Holbach, 34, 861.

some twenty-five at the University of Leyden at that time.[3] Already at the age of twenty-three Holbach was writing very good English, and all his life he was a friend of Englishmen and English ideas. His friendship for Wilkes, then a lad of nineteen, lasted all his life and increased in intimacy and dignity. The two letters following are of interest because they are the only documents we have bearing on Holbach's early manhood. They reveal a certain sympathy and feeling—rather gushing to be sure—quite unlike anything in his later writings, and quite out of line with the supposedly cold temper of a materialist and an atheist.[4]

HOLBACH TO WILKES

HÉEZE Aug. 9, 1746

Dearest Friend

I should not have felt by half enough the pleasure your kind letter gave me, If I had words to express it; I never doubted of your friendship, nor I hope do you know me so little as to doubt of mine, but your letter is full of such favorable sentiments to me that I must own I cannot repay them but by renewing to you the entire gift of my heart that has been yours ever since heaven favour'd me with your acquaintance. I need not tell you the sorrow our parting gave me, in vain Philosophy cried aloud nature was still stronger and the philosopher was forced to yield to the friend, even now I feel the wound is not cur'd. Therefore no more of that— *Hope* is my motto. Telling me you are happy you make me so but in the middle of your happiness you dont forget your friend, What flattering thought to me! Such are the

[3] Carlyle, Rev. Dr. A., *Autobiography*, ed. Burton, Boston, 1861, p. 137 sq. for Holbach's English friends mentioned in his letters to Wilkes.

[4] These letters, contrary to modern usage, are printed with all the peculiarities of eighteenth century orthography. It was felt that they would lose their quaintness and charm if Holbach's somewhat fantastic English were trifled with or his spelling, capitalization and punctuation modernized.

charms of friendship every event is shar'd and nothing nor even the greatest intervals are able to interrupt the happy harmony of truly united minds. I left Leyden about 8 or 10 days after you but before my departure I thought myself obliged to let Mr Dowdenwell know what you told me, he has seen the two letters Mr Johnson had received and I have been mediator of ye peace made betwixt the 2 parties, I don't doubt but you have seen by this time Messrs Bland & Weatherill who were to set out for Engelland the same week I parted with them. When I was leaving Leyden Mr Vernon happen'd to tell me he had a great mind to make a trip to Spa. So my uncles' estate being on ye road I desir'd him to come along with me, he has been here a week and went on afterwards in his journey, at my arrival here, I found that General Count Palfi with an infinite number of military attendants had taken possession of my uncles' house, and that the 16 thous^{d} men lately come from Germany to strengthen the allies army, commanded by Count Bathiani and that had left ye neighborhood of Breda a few days before and was come to Falkenswert (where you have past in your journey to Spa) one hour from hence. Prince Charles arrived here the same day from Germany to take ye command of the allies, the next Day the whole army amounting to 70th^{d} men went on towards the county of Liège to prevent the French from beseiging Namur, I hear now that the two armies are only one hour from another, so we expect very soon the news of a great battle but not without fear, Count Saxes army being, by all account of hundred ten thou$^{d.}$ men besides. Prince Counti's army of 50 th$^{d.}$ this latter General is now employ'd at the siege of Charleroy, that can't resist a long while, it is a report that the King of France is arrived in his army, I hope this long account will entertain you for want of news papers: Mr. Dowdeswell being left alone of our club at Leyden I Desir'd him to come and spend with me the time of his vacations here, which proposal I hope he will accept and be here next week. What happy triumvirat would be ours if you were to join: but that is impossible at present; however those who cant enjoy reality are fond of feeding their fancies with agreable Dreams and charming pictures; that helps a little to sooth the sorrow of absence and makes one expect with more pati[ence] till fortune allows him to put in execution the cherish'd systems he has been fed upon fore some [time] I shall expect with great many thanks the books you are to send me; it will be for me a dubble pleasure to read them, being of your choice which I value as much as it deserves, and looking at them as upon a new proof of your benevolence, as to those I design'd to get from Paris for you, I heard I could not get them before my uncles' return hither all commerce being stopt by the way betwixt this country and France.

A few days before my departure from Leyden I receiv'd a letter from M[r] Freeman from Berlin, he seams vastly pleas'd with our Germany, and chiefly with Hambourg where a beautiful lady has taken in his heart the room of poor M[ss.] Vitsiavius, my prophesy was just; traveling seems to have alter'd a good deal his melancholy disposition as I may conjecture by his way of writing. He desired his service to you. As to me, Idleness renders me every day more philosopher every passion is languishing within me, I retain but one in a warm degree, viz, friendship in which you share no small part. I took a whim to study a little Physic accordingly I purchased several books in that Way, and my empty hours here are employ'd with them. I am sure your time will be much better employ'd at Alesbury you'll find there a much nobler entertainment Cupid is by far Lovlier than Esculapius, however I shall not envy your happiness, in the Contrary I wish that all your desires be crown'd with success, that a Passion that proves fatal to great many of men be void of sorrow for you, that all the paths of love be spred over with flowers in one Word that you may not address in vain to the charming M[ss.] M. I am almost tempted to fall in love with that unknown beauty, 't would not be quite like Don Quixotte for your liking to her would be for me a very strong prejudice of her merit, which the poor Knight had not in his love for Dulcinea.

I shall not ask your pardon for the length of this letter I am sure friendship will forgive the time I steal to Love however I cannot give up so easily a conversation with a true friend with whom I fancy to speak yet in one of those delightfull evening walks at Leyden. It is a dream, I own it, but it is so agreable one to me that nothing but reality could be compared to the pleasure I feel: let me therefore insist a little more upon't and travel with my Letter, we are gone! I think to be at Alesbury! there I see my Dear Wilkes! What a Flurry of Panions! Joy! fear of a second parting! what charming tears! what sincere Kisses!—but time flows and the end of this Love is now as unwelcome to me, as would be to another to be awaken'd in the middle of a Dream wherein he is going to enjoy a beloved mistress; the enchantment ceases, the delightfull images vanish, and nothing is left to me but friendship, which is of all my possessions the fairest, and the surest, I am most sincerely Dear Wilkes

Your affectionate friend
and humble servant
DE HOLBACH

Heze the 9th august 1746 N. S.

I shall expect with impatience the letter you are to write me from Alesbury. Will it be here very soon!

HOLBACH TO WILKES

[HÉEZE Dec. 3rd. 1746]

Dearest Wilkes

During a little voyage I have made into Germany I have received your charming letter of the 8th. September O. S. the many affairs I have been busy with for these 3 months has hindered me hitherto from returning to you as speedy an answer as I should have done. I know too much your kindness for me to make any farther apology and I hope you are enough acquainted with the sincerety of my friendship towards you to adscribe my fault to forgetfulness or want of gratitude be sure, Dear friend, that such a disposition will allways be unknown to me in regard to you. I don't doubt but you will be by this time returned at

London, the winter season being an obstacle to the pleasures you have enjoyed following ye Letter at Alesbury during the last Autumn. I must own I have felt a good deal of pride when you gave me the kind assurance that love has not made you forget an old friend, I need not tell you my disposition. I hope you know it well enough and like my friendship for you has no bounds I want expressions to show it. Mr Dowdeswell has been so good as to let me enjoy his company here in the month of August, and returned to Leyden to pursue his studies in the middle of September. We often wished your company and made sincere libations to you with burgundy and Champaigne I had a few weeks there after I set out for Germany where I expected to spend the whole winter but the sudden death of my Uncle's Steward has forced me to come back here to put in order the affairs of this estate, I don't know how long I shall be obliged to stay in the meanwhile I act pretty well the part of a County Squire, id est, hunting, shooting, fishing, walking every day without to lay aside the ever charming conversation of Horace Virgil Homer and all our noble friends of the Elysian fields. They are allways faithfull to me, with their aid I find very well how to employ my time, but I want in this country a true bosom friend like my dear Wilkes to converse with, but my pretenssions are too high, for every abode with such a company would be heaven for me.

I perceive by your last letter that your hopes are very like to succeed by M^{ss} Mead, you are sure that every happines that can befall to you will make me vastly happy. I beseech you therefore to let me know everytime how far you are gone, I take it to be a very good omen for you, that your lovely mistress out of compliance has vouchsafed to learn a harsh high-dutch name, which would otherwise have made her starttle, at the very hearing of it. I am very thankful for her kind desire of seeing me in Engelland which I dont wish the less but you know my circumstances enough, to guess that I cannot follow my inclinations. I have not heard hitherto anything about the books you have been so kind as to send me over by the opportunity of a friend. I have wrote about it to M^{srs} Conrad et Bouwer of Rotterdam, they answered that they were not yet there. Nevertheless I am very much oblided to you for your kindness and wish to find very soon the opportunity of my revenge. Mr Dowderswell complains very much of Mrs Bland and Weatherill, having not heard of them since their departure from Leyden. I desire my compliments to Mr Dyer and all our old acquaintances. Pray be so good as to direct your first letter under the covert of Mr Dowderwell at M^{s} Alliaume's at Leyden he shall send it to me over immediately, no more at Mr Van Sprang's like you used to do. I wish to know if Mr Lyson since his return to his native country, continues in his peevish cross temper. If you have any news besides I'll be glad to hear them by your next which I expect very soon.

About politicks I cannot tell you anything at present, you have heard enough by this time the fatal battle fought near Liège in 8^{ber} last; everybody has little hopes of the Congress of Breda, the Austrian and Piedmontese are entered into provence, which is not as difficult as to maintain themselves therein, I wish a speedy peace would enable us both to see the rejoicings that will attend the marriage of the Dauphin of France with a Princess of Saxony. I have heard that peace is made between England and Spain, which you ought to know better than I. We fear very much for the next campaign the siege of Maestrich in our neighborhood. These are all the news I know. I'll tell you another that you have known a long while viz. that nobody is with more sincerity My Dear Wilkes

Your faithfull humble Servant and Friend

HOLBACH

Heeze the 3^{d} X^{ber} 1746 ns

By 1750 Holbach was established in Paris as a young man of the world. His fortune, his learning, his sociability attracted the younger literary set toward him. In 1749 he was already holding his Thursday dinners which later became so famous. Among his early friends were Diderot, Rousseau and Grimm. With them he took the side of the Italian *Opera buffa* in the famous musical quarrel of 1752, and published two witty brochures ridiculing French music.[5] He was an art connoisseur and bought Oudry's *Chienne allaitant ses petits*, the *chef d'oeuvre* of the Salon of 1753.[6] During these years he was hard at work at his chosen sciences of chemistry and mineralogy. In 1752 he published in a huge volume in quarto with excellent plates, a translation of Antonio Neri's *Art of Glass making*, and in 1753 a translation of Wallerius' *Mineralogy*. On July 26, 1754, the Academy of Berlin made him a foreign associate in recognition of his scholarly attainments in Natural History,[7] and later he was elected to the Academies of St. Petersburg and Mannheim.

All that was now lacking to this brilliant young man was an attractive wife to rule over his salon. His friends urged him to wed, and in 1753 he married Mlle. Basile-Genevieve-Susanne d'Aine, daughter of "Maître Marius-Jean-Baptiste Nicolas d'Aine, conseiller au Roi en son grand conseil, associé externe de l'Acad. des sciences et belles letters de Prusse."[8] M. d'Aine was also Maître des Requêtes and a man of means. Mme. d'Holbach was a very charming and gracious woman and Holbach's good fortune seemed complete when suddenly Mme. d'Holbach died from a most loathsome and painful disease in the summer of 1754. Holbach was heart-broken and took a trip through the provinces with his friend Grimm, to whom he was much attached, to distract his mind from his grief. He returned in the early winter and the next year (1755) got a special dispensation from the Pope to marry his deceased wife's sister, Mlle. Charlotte-Susanne d'Aine. By her he had four children, two sons and two daughters. The first, Charles-Marius, was born about the middle of August, 1757, and baptized in Saint-

---

[5] See Chap. II and Bibliography, Pt. I, for these and his other works.

[6] Grimm *Cor. Lit.*, Vol. II, p. 283.

[7] *Gazette de France*, Aug. 10, 1754.

[8] Jal, *Dict. Critique*, p. 685.

Germain-l'Auxerrois, Aug. 22. He inherited the family title and was a captain in the regiment of the Schomberg-Dragons.[9] The first daughter was born towards the end of 1758 and the second about the middle of Jan., 1760.[10] The elder married the Marquis de Châtenay and the younger the Marquis de Nolivos, "Captaine au régiment de la Seurre, Dragons." Their Majesties the King and Queen and the Royal Family signed their marriage contract May 27, 1781.[11] Of the second son there seem to be no traces. Holbach's mother-in-law, Madame d'Aine, was a very interesting old woman as she is pictured in Diderot's *Mémoires*, and there was a brother-in-law, "Messire Marius-Jean-Baptiste-Nicholas d'Aine, chevalier, conseiller du roi en ses conseils, Maître des requêtes honoraire de son hôtel, intendant de justice, police, et finances de la généralité de Tours," who lived in rue Saint Dominique, paroisse Saint-Sulpice. There was in Holbach's household for a long time an old Scotch surgeon, a homeless, misanthropic old fellow by the name of Hope, of whom Diderot gives a most interesting account.[12] These are the

---

[9] His career is somewhat doubtful. He travelled in Italy in 1779 and Abbé Galiani, an old friend of Holbach's, got a very agreeable impression of him. John Wilkes, in a letter to his daughter in 1781, seems to imply that he had not turned out very well, and hopes that the baron's second son will make good the deficiencies of the first. In 1806 he published a translation of Weiland's *Oberon* or *Huon de Bordeaux* which went thru another edition in 1825, but those are the only details that have come to light

[10] Diderot, in writing to Mlle Volland Sep. 17, 1760 says: "On nourrit, à Chenvières, les deux filles de Madame d'Holbach. L'aînée est belle comme un chérubin; c'est un visage rond, de grands yeux bleus, des levres fines, une bouche riante, la peau la plus blanche et la plus animée, des cheveux châtains qui ceignent un très joli front. La cadette est un peloton d'embonpoint où l'on ne distingue encore que du blanc et du vermillon.

[11] Gazette de France, June 1, 1781.

[12] Holbach's intendant was [a] Jew, Berlise. After his death several of his old servants Vincent, David, and Plocque, contested Holbach's will, in which they thought they were legatees. The case was in the courts for several years and was finally decided against them. Douarche, *Les tribunaux civil de Paris pendant la révolution*, Paris, 1905, Vol. I., pp. 141, 261, 325, 689.

only names we have of the personnel of Holbach's household. His town house was in the rue Royale, butte Saint-Roch. It was here that for an almost unbroken period of forty years he gave his Sunday and Thursday dinners. The latter day was known to the more intimate set of encyclopedists as the *jour du synagogue*. Here the *église philosophique* met regularly to discuss its doctrines and publish its propaganda of radicalism.

Holbach had a very pleasant country seat, the château of Grandval, now in the arrondisement of Boissy St. Léger at Sucy-en-Brie. It is pleasantly situated in the valley of a little stream, the Morbra, which flows into the Marne. The property was really the estate of Mme. d'Aine who lived with the Holbachs. Here the family and their numerous guests passed the late summer and fall. Here Diderot spent weeks at a time working on the Encyclopedia, dining, and walking on the steep slopes of the Marne with congenial companions. To him we are indebted for our intimate knowledge of Grandval and its inhabitants, their slightest doings and conversations; and as Danou has well said, if we were to wish ourselves back in any past age we should choose with many others the mid-eighteenth century and the charming society of Paris and Grandval.[13]

Holbach's life, in common with that of most philosophers, offers no events, except that he came near being killed in the crush and riot in the rue Royale that followed the fire at the Dauphin's wedding in 1770.[14] He was never an official personage. His entire life was spent in study, writing and conversation with his friends. He traveled very little; the world came to him, to the *Café de l'Europe*, as Abbé Galiani called Paris. From time to time Holbach went to Contrexéville for his gout and once to England to visit David Garrick; but he disliked England very thoroughly and was glad to get back to Paris. The events of his life in so far as there were any, were his relations

[13] Avézac-Lavigne, *Diderot*, p. 5.

[14] *Critica*, Vol. I, p. 48, note.

with people. He knew intimately practically all the great men of his century, except Montesquieu and Voltaire, who were off the stage before his day.[15] Holbach's most intimate and life-long friend among the great figures of the century was Diderot, of whom Rousseau said, "À la distance de quelques siècles du moment où il a vécu, Diderot paraîtra un homme prodigieux; on regardera de loin cette tête universelle avec une admiration mêlée d'étonnement, comme nous regardons aujourd'hui la tête des Platon et des Aristote."[16] All his contemporaries agreed that nothing was so charged with divine fire as the conversation of Diderot. Gautherin, in his fine bronze of him on the Place Saint-Germain-des-Près, seems to have caught the spirit of his talk and has depicted him as he might have sat in the midst of Holbach's society, of which he was the inspiration and the soul. Holbach backed Diderot financially in his great literary and scientific undertaking and provided articles for the Encyclopedia on chemistry and natural science. Diderot had a high opinion of his erudition and said of him, "Quelque système que forge mon imagination, je suis sur que mon ami d'Holbach me trouve des faits et des autorités pour le justifier."[17] Opinions differ in regard to the intellectual influence of these men upon each other. Diderot was without doubt the greater thinker, but Holbach stated his atheism with far greater clarity and Diderot gave his sanction to it by embellishing Holbach's books with a few

---

[15] He met Voltaire in Paris in 1778, however, and Naigeon relates that Voltaire greeted him very cordially and said that he had long desired to make his acquaintance.

[16] Collignon, *Diderot*, p. 1.

["From the perspective of a few centuries after his life, Diderot will appear a prodigious man; people will admire from afar this polymath (literally 'universal head') with admiration mixed with wonder, just as we now gaze upon those of Plato and Aristotle."]

[17] Avézac-Lavigne, *Diderot*, p. 75, note.

["Whatever system my imagination dreamt up, I'm sure my friend Holbach found me the facts and authorities to support it."]

eloquent pages of his own. Diderot said to Sir Samuel Romilly in 1781, "Il faut *sabrer* la théologie,"[18] and died in 1784 in the belief that complete infidelity was the first step toward philosophy. Five years later Holbach was buried by his side in the crypt of the Chapel of the Virgin behind the high altar in Saint-Roch. No tablet marks their tombs, and although repeated investigations have been made no light has been thrown on the exact position of their burial place. According to Diderot's daughter, Mme. Vandeuil, their entire correspondence has been destroyed or lost.[19]

Holbach's relations with Rousseau were less harmonious. The account of their mutual misunderstandings contained in the *Confessions*, in a letter by Cerutti in the *Journal de Paris* Dec. 2, 1789, and in private letters of Holbach's to Hume, Garrick, and Wilkes, is a long and tiresome tale. The author of *Eclaircissements relatifs à la publication des confessions de Rousseau...* (Paris, 1789) blames the *club holbachique* for their treatment of Rousseau, but the fault seems to lie on both sides. According to Rousseau's account, Holbach sought his friendship and for a few years he was one of Holbach's society. But, after the success of the *Devin du Village* in 1753, the *holbachiens* turned against him out of jealousy of his genius as a composer. Visions of a dark plot against him rose before his fevered and sensitive imagination, and after 1756 he left the Society of the Encyclopedists, never to return. Holbach, on the other hand, while admitting rather questionable treatment of Rousseau, never speaks of any personal injury on his part, and bewails the fact that "l'homme le plus éloquent s'est rendu ainsi l'homme le plus anti-littéraire, et l'homme le plus sensible s'est rendu le plus anti-social."[20] He did warn Hume against taking him to England,

---

[18] Romilly, *Memoirs*, Vol. I, p. 179.

["We must *slash* theology."]

[19] Diderot, *Oeuvres*, Vol. I, p. lxvi, note.

[20] Journal de Paris, Dec. 2, 1789.

and in a letter to Wilkes predicted the quarrel that took place shortly after. In writing to Garrick[21] he says some hard but true things about Rousseau, who on his part never really defamed Holbach but depicted him as the virtuous atheist under the guise of Wolmar in the *Nouvelle Heloïse*. Their personal incompatibility is best explained on the grounds of the radical differences in their temperaments and types of mind and by the fact that Rousseau was too sensitive to get on with anybody for any great length of time.

Two other great Frenchmen, Buffon and d'Alembert, were for a time members of Holbach's society, but, for reasons that are not altogether clear, gradually withdrew. Grimm suggests that Buffon did not find the young philosophers sufficiently deferential to him and to the authorized powers, and feared for his dignity,—and safety, in their company. D'Alembert, on the other hand, was a recluse by nature, and, after giving up his editorship on the Encyclopedia, easily dropped out of Diderot's society and devoted himself to Mlle. Lespinasse and Mme. Geoffrin. Holbach and Helvetius were life-long friends and spent much time together reading at Helvetius's country place at Voré. After his death in 1774, Holbach frequented Mme. Helvetius' salon where he knew and deeply influenced Volney, Cabanis, de Tracy, and the first generation of the Ideologists who continued his and Helvetius' philosophical doctrines. Among the other Frenchmen of the day who were on intimate relations with Holbach and frequented his salon were La Condamine, Condillac, Condorcet, Turgot, Morellet, Raynal, Grimm, Marmontel, Colardeau, Saurin, Suard, Saint-Lambert, Thomas, Duclos, Chastellux, Boulanger, Darcet, Roux, Rouelle, Barthès, Venel, Leroy, Damilaville, Naigeon, Lagrange and lesser names,—but well known in Paris in the eighteenth century,—

["The most eloquent man has thus become the most anti-literary man; and the most sensitive man, the most anti-social."]

[21] See appendix, p. 78, p. 81.

d'Alinville, Chauvelin, Desmahis, Gauffecourt, Margency, de Croismare, de Pezay, Coyer, de Valory, Charnoi, not to mention a host of others.

Among Holbach's most intimate English friends were Hume, Garrick, Wilkes, Sterne, Gibbon, Horace Walpole, Adam Smith, Benjamin Franklin, Dr. Priestley, Lord Shelburne, Gen. Barré, Gen. Clark, Sir James MacDonald, Dr. Gem, Messrs. Stewart, Demster, Fordyce, Fitzmaurice, Foley, etc. Holbach addressed a letter to Hume in 1762, before making his acquaintance, in which he expressed his admiration of his philosophy and the desire to know him personally.[22] In 1764 Hume came to Paris as secretary of the British Embassy and immediately called on Holbach and became a regular frequenter of his salon. It was to Holbach that he wrote first on the outbreak of his quarrel with Rousseau and they corresponded at length in regard to the publication of the *Exposé succinct*, which was to justify Hume in the eyes of the French. Hume and Holbach had much in common intellectually, although the latter was far more thoroughgoing in his repudiation of Theism.

David Garrick and his wife were frequent visitors at the rue Royale on their trips to Paris where they were very much liked by Holbach's society. Nothing is more cordial or gracious than the compliments passed between them in their subsequent correspondence. There are two published letters from Holbach in Mr. Hedgecock's recent study of Garrick and his French friends, excellent examples of the happy spontaneity and sympathy that were characteristic of French sociability in the eighteenth century.[23] Holbach in turn spent several months with Garrick at Hampton.

Holbach's early friendship for Wilkes has already been mentioned. Wilkes spent a great deal of time in Paris on the occasion of his exiles from England and became very intimate

---

[22] See appendix, p. 79.

[23] See appendix, p. 78.

with Holbach. They corresponded up to the very end of Holbach's life and there was a constant interchange of friendly offices between them.[24] Miss Wilkes, who spent much time in Paris, was a very good friend of Mme. Holbach and Mlle. Helvetius. Adam Smith often dined at Holbach's with Turgot and the economists; Gibbon also found his dinners agreeable except for the dogmatism of the atheists; Walpole resented it also and kept away. Priestley seems to have gotten on very well, although the philosophers found his materialism and unitarianism a trifle inconsistent. It was at Holbach's that Shelburne met Morellet with whom he carried on a long and serious correspondence on economics. There seem to be no details of Holbach's relations with Franklin, who was evidently more assiduous at the salon of Mme. Helvetius whom he desired to marry.

Holbach's best friend among the Italians was Abbé Galiani, secretary of the Neapolitan Embassy, who spent ten years in the salons of Paris. After his return to Naples his longing for Paris led him to a voluminous correspondence with his French friends including Holbach. A few of their letters are extant. Beccaria also came to Paris at the invitation of the translator of his *Crimes and Punishments*, Abbé Morellet, made on behalf of Holbach and his society. Beccaria and his friend Veri, who accompanied him, had long been admirers of French philosophy, and the Frenchmen found much to admire in Beccaria's book. One *avocat-général*, M. Servan of the Parlement of Bordeaux, a friend of Holbach's, tried to put his reforms in practice and shared the fate of most reformers. Holbach was also in correspondence with Beccaria, and one of his letters has been published in M. Landry's recent study of Beccaria.

Among the other Italians whom Holbach befriended were Paulo Frizi, the mathematician; Dr. Gatti; Pincini, the musician; and Mme. Riccoboni, ex-actress and novelist; whose lively

---

[24] See pp. 6 sq. and appendix pp. 83 sq.

correspondence with Garrick whom she met at Holbach's sheds much light on the social relations of the century.

Among the other foreigners who were friends or acquaintances of Holbach were his fellow countrymen, Frederich Melchon Grimm, like himself a naturalized Frenchman and the bosom friend of Diderot; Meister, his collaborator in the *Literary Correspondence*; Kohant, a Bohemian musician, composer, of the *Bergère des Alpes* and Mme. Holbach's lute-teacher; Baron Gleichen, Comte de Creutz, Danish and Scandinavian diplomats; and a number of German nobles; the hereditary princes of Brunswick and Saxe Gotha, Baron Alaberg, afterwards elector of Mayence, Baron Schomberg and Baron Studitz.

Among the well known women of the century Holbach was most intimate with Mme. d'Epinay, who became a very good friend of Mme. Holbach's and was present at the birth of her first son, and, in her will, left her a portrait by Rembrandt. He was also a friend of Mme. Geoffrin, attended her salon, and knew Mlle. de Lespinasse, Mme. Houderot and most of the important women of the day.

There are excellent sources from which to form an estimate of this man whose house was the social centre of the century. Just after Holbach's death on January 21, 1789, Naigeon, his literary agent, who had lived on terms of the greatest intimacy with him for twenty-four years, wrote a long eulogy which filled the issue of the *Journal de Paris* for Feb. 9. There was another letter to the *Journal* on Feb. 12. Grimm's *Correspondance Littéraire* for March contains a long account of him by Meister, and there are other notices in contemporary memoirs such as Morellet's and Marmontel's. All these accounts agree in picturing him as the most admirable of men.

It must be remembered that Holbach always enjoyed what was held to be a considerable fortune in his day. From his estates in Westphalia he had a yearly income of 60,000 *livres* which he spent in entertaining. This freedom from economic pressure gave him leisure to devote his time to his chosen intellectual pursuits and to his friends. He was a universally learned man. He knew French, German, English, Italian and Latin extremely well and had a fine private library of about three thousand works often of several volumes each, in these languages and in Greek and Hebrew. The catalogue of this library was published by Debure in 1789. It would be difficult to imagine a more comprehensive and complete collection of its size. He had also a rich collection of drawings by the best masters, fine pictures of which he was a connoisseur, bronzes, marbles, porcelains and a natural history cabinet, so in vogue in those days, containing some very valuable specimens. He was one of the most learned men of his day in natural science, especially chemistry and mineralogy, and to his translations from the best German scientific works is largely due the spread of scientific learning in France in the eighteenth century. Holbach was also very widely read in English theology and philosophy of the seventeenth and eighteenth centuries and derived his anti-theological inspiration from these two sources. To this vast fund of learning, he joined an extreme modesty and simplicity. He sought no academic honors, published all his works anonymously, and, had it not been for the pleasure he took in communicating his ideas to his friends, no one would have suspected his great erudition. He had an extraordinary memory and the reputation of never forgetting anything of interest. This plenitude of information, coupled with his easy and pleasant manner of talking, made his society much sought after. Naigeon said of him (in his preface to the works of Lagrange):

Personne n'était plus communicatif que M. le baron d'Holbach; personne ne prenait aux progrès de la raison un intérêt plus vif, plus sincère, et ne s'occupait avec plus de zèle et l'activité des moyens de les accélérer.

Également versé dans la plupart des matières sur lesquelles il importe le plus à des êtres raisonnables d'avoir une opinion arrêtée, M. le baron d'Holbach portait dans leur discussion un jugement sain, une logique sévère, et une analyse exacte et précise. Quelque fut l'objet de ses entretiens avec ses amis, ou même avec des indifférens, tels qu'en offrent plus ou moins toutes les sociétés; il inspirait sans effort à ceux qui l'écoutaient l'enthousiasme de l'art ou de la science dont il parlait; et on ne le quittait jamais sans regretter de n'avoir pas cultivé la branche particulière de connaissances qui avait fait le sujet de la conversation, sans désirer d'être plus instruit, plus éclairé, et surtout sans admirer la claret, la justesse de son esprit, et l'ordre dans lequel il savait présenter ses idées.[25]

This virtue of communicativeness, of *sociabilité*, Holbach carried into all the relations of life. He was always glad to lend or give his books to anyone who could make use of them. "Je suis riche," he used to say, "mais je ne vois dans la fortune qu'un instrument de plus pour opérer le bien plus promptement et plus efficacement."[26] In fact Holbach's whole principle of life and action was to increase the store of human well being. And he did this without any religious motive whatsoever. As Julie says of Wolmar in *La Nouvelle Heloïse*, "Il fait le bien sans espoir de récompense, il est plus vertueux, plus désintéressé que nous."[27]

---

[25] [No one was a better communicator than Baron d'Holbach; no one took a keener, more sincere interest in the progress of reason, nor applied themselves with more zeal and activity to the means of accelerating it.

Equally versed in the majority of subjects on which it most matters to beings of reason to have a firm opinion, Baron d'Holbach brought to their discussion sound judgment, severe logic, and accurate and precise analysis. Whatever the subject of his talks, either with his friends, or with the indifferent, such as one finds in nearly all societies; he effortlessly inspired his listeners with enthusiasm for the art or science of which he spoke, and they never left him without regret for not having cultivated the particular branch of knowledge that had been the subject of conversation, without wishing to be more educated, more enlightened, and above all without admiring the clarity, the soundness of his mind, and the order in which he knew how to present his ideas.]

[26] ["I'm rich," he used to say, "but I only see fortune as an instrument to do good more quickly and effectively."]

[27] ["He does good without hope of reward, he is more virtuous, more unselfish than us."]

There are many recorded instances of Holbach's gracious benevolence. As he said to Helvetius, "Vous êtes brouillé avec tous ceux que vous avez obligé, mais j'ai gardé tous mes amis."[28] Holbach had the faculty of attaching people to him. Diderot tells how at the Salon of 1753 after Holbach had bought Oudry's famous picture, all the collectors who had passed it by came to him and offered him twice what he paid for it. Holbach went to find the artist to ask him permission to cede the picture to his profit, but Oudry refused, saying that he was only too happy that his best work belonged to the man who was the first to appreciate it. Instances of Holbach's liberality to Kohant, a poor musician, and to Suard, a poor literary man, are to be found in the pages of Diderot and Meister, and his constant generosity to his friends is a commonplace in their Memoirs and Correspondence. Only Rousseau was ungrateful enough to complain that Holbach's free-handed gifts insulted his poverty. His kindness to Lagrange, a young literary man whom he rescued from want, has been well told by M. Naigeon in the preface to the works of Lagrange (p. xviii).

But perhaps the most touching instances of Holbach's benevolence are his relations with the peasants of Contrexéville, one of which was published in the *Journal de Lecture*, 1775, the other in an anonymous letter to the *Journal de Paris*, Feb. 12, 1789. The first concerns the reconciliation of two old peasants who, not wanting to go to court, brought their differences to their respected friend for a settlement. Nothing is more simple and beautiful than this homely tale as told in a letter of Holbach's to a friend of his. The second, which John Wilkes said ought to be written in letters of gold, deserves to be reproduced as a whole.

L'éloge funèbre que M. Naigeon a consacré à la mémoire de M. le Baron d'Holbach suffit pour donner une idée juste de ses lumières, mais le hasard m'a mis à portée de les juger encore

---

[28] ["You are confused by all those you have helped, but I have kept all my friends."]

mieux. J'ai vu M. le Baron d'Holbach dans deux voyages que j'ai faits aux eaux de Contrexéville. S'occuper de sa souffrance et de sa guérison, c'est le soin de chaque malade. M. le Baron d'Holbach devenait le médecin, l'ami, le consolateur de quiconque venait aux eaux et il semblait bien moins occupé de ses infirmités que de celles des autres. Lorsque des malades indigens manquaient de secours, ou pécuniaires ou curatifs, il les leur procurait avec un plaisir qui lui faisait plus de bien que les eaux. Je me promenais un soir avec lui sur une hauteur couverte d'un massif de bois qui fait perspective de loin et près duquel s'élève un petit Hermitage. Là, demeure un cénobite qui n'a de revenu que les aumônes de ceux dont il reçoit les visites. Nous acquittâmes chacun notre dette hospitalière. En prenant congé de l'Hermite, M. le Baron d'Holbach me dit de le précéder un instant et qu'il allait me suivre. Je le précédai, et comme il ne me suivait pas je m'arrêtai, pour l'attendre sur un terte exhaussé d'où l'on découvre tout le pays. Je contemplais le canton que je dominais, plongé dans une douce rêverie. J'en fus tiré par des cris et je me retournai vers l'endroit d'òu ils partaient. Je vis M. le Baron d'Holbach environné d'une vieille femme et de deux villageois, l'un vieux comme elle et l'autre jeune. Tous trois, les larmes aux yeux, l'embrassaient hautement. Allez vous-en donc, s'écrait M. le Baron d'Holbach; laissez moi, on m'attend, ne me suivez pas, adieu; je reviendrai l'année prochaine. En me voyant arriver vers eux, les trois personnes reconnaissantes disparurent. Je lui demandai le sujet de tant de bénédictions. Ce jeune paysan que vous avez vu s'etait engagé, j'ai obtenu de son colonel sa liberté en payant les cents écus prescrits par l'ordonnance. Il est amoureux d'une jeune paysanne aussi pauvre que lui, je viens d'acheter pour eux un petit bien qui m'a coûté huit cent francs. Le vieux père est perclus, aux deux bras, de rhumatismes, je lui ai fourni trois boîtes du baume des Valdejeots, si estimé en ce pays-ci. La vieille mère est sujetté à des maux d'estomac, et je lui ai apporté un pot de confection d'hyacinthe. Ils travaillaient dans le champ, voisin du bois, je suis allé les voir tandis que vous marchiez en avant. Ils m'ont suivi malgré moi. Ne parlez de cela à personne. On dirait que je veux faire le généreux et le bon philosophe, mais je ne suis que humain, et mes charités sont la plus agréable dépense de mes voyages.[29]

This humanity of Holbach's is the very keynote of his character and of his intellectual life as well. As M. Walferdin has said, the denial of the supernatural was for him the base of all virtue, and resting on this principle, he exemplified social

---

[29] [The eulogy that Mr. Naigeon dedicated to the memory of Baron d'Holbach is sufficient to give a fair idea of his merits, but chance gave me the opportunity to judge them even better. I saw the Baron d'Holbach on two trips I made to the waters of Contrexéville. Every patient is preoccupied with their own suffering and sickness. Baron d'Holbach became the doctor, the friend, the consoler of anyone who came to the waters and he seemed much less concerned with his own infirmities than those of others. When poor patients lacked help, either financial or curative, he assisted them, the pleasure of which did him far more good than the waters. I was walking one evening with him on a wooded hill with panoramic views, near which stands a small Hermitage. There dwells a monk whose only income is from the alms of his visitors. We each paid our debt of hospitality. Taking leave of the Hermit, Baron d'Holbach told me to precede him for a bit and he would follow me. I walked on, and as he didn't follow me I stopped to wait on a high lookout, from which one can see the entire country. I gazed at the countryside below, lost in a sweet reverie. I was awakened by cries so I went back in the direction they came from. I saw the Baron d'Holbach surrounded by an old woman and two village men, one as old as she and the other young. All three, in tears, were embracing him enthusiastically. 'Get away with you', cried Baron d'Holbach, 'let me go! Someone's waiting for me, stop following me, goodbye! I'll be back next year.' Seeing me coming towards them, the three grateful people disappeared. I asked him the reason for so many blessings. 'The young peasant you saw had been enlisted, I got his colonel to release him by paying the hundred crowns prescribed by the regulations. He is in love with a peasant girl as poor as him, I just bought them a small property which cost me eight hundred francs. His old father is crippled in both arms with rheumatism, I brought him three boxes of Valdejeots balm, much prized in this country. His old mother is prone to stomach upset and I brought her a pot of hyacinth remedy. They were working in the field next to the wood, I went to see them while you carried on. They followed me against my will. Don't tell anyone! People would say I want to play the benefactor and doer of good deeds, but I am only human, and my charities are the most enjoyable expense of my travels.']

qualities that do the greatest honor to human nature. He and Madame Holbach are the only conspicuous examples of conjugal fidelity and happiness among all the people that one has occasion to mention in a study of the intellectual and literary circles of the eighteenth century. They were devoted to each other, to their children and to their friends. Considering the traits of Holbach's character that have been cited, there can scarcely be two opinions in regard to completeness with which he realized his ideal of humanity and sociability. M. Naigeon has well summed up in a few words Holbach's relation to the only duties that he recognized, "He was a good husband, a good father and a good friend."

CHAPTER II.
HOLBACH'S WORKS.

Holbach's published works, with the exception of a few scattered ones, may be divided into three classes, viz., translations of German scientific works, translations of English deistical writings, and his own works on theology, philosophy, politics and morals. Those which fall into none of these categories can be dealt with very summarily. They are:

1. Two pamphlets on the musical dispute of 1752; *Lettre à une dame d'un certain âge sur l'état présent de l'Opéra*, (8vo, pp. 11) and *Arrêt rendu à l'amphithéâtre de l'Opéra*, (8vo, pp. 16,) both directed against French music and in line with Grimm's *Petit Prophète* and Rousseau's *Lettre sur la musique française*.

2. A translation in prose of Akenside's *The Pleasures of Imagination* (Paris, 1759, 8vo).

3. A translation of Swift's *History of the Reign of Queen Anne* in collaboration with M. Eidous (Amsterdam, 1765, 12mo, pp. xxiv + 416).

4. Translations of an Ode on Human Life and a Hymn to the Sun in the Variétés littéraires (1768).

5. Articles on natural science in the Encyclopédie and article Prononciation des langues in the Dictionnaire de Grammaire of the Encyclopédie méthodique.

6. Translation of Wallerius' *Agriculture reduced to its true principles* (Paris, 1774, 12mo).

7. Two Facéties philosophiques published in Grimm's Correspondence Littéraire. L'Abbé et le Rabbin, and Essai sur l'art de ramper, à l'usage des courtisans.

8. Parts of Raynal's Histoire philosophique des deux Indes.

9. Notes to Lagrange's *Vie de Senèque.*

Holbach's translations of German scientific works are as follows: (Complete titles to be found in Bibliography, Pt. I.)

1. *Art de la Verrerie de Neri, Merret, et Kunckel* (Paris, Durand, 1752). Original work in Italian. Latin translation by Christopher Merret. German translation by J. Kunckel of Löwenstern. Holbach's translation comprises the seven books of Antionio Neri, Merret's notes on Neri, Kunckel's observations on both these authors, his own experiments and others relative to glass-making. The translation was dedicated to Malesherbes who had desired to see the best German scientific works published in French. In his *Préface du Traducteur* Holbach writes:

L'envie de me rendre utile, dont tout citoyen doit être animé, m'a fait entreprendre l'ouvrage que je présente au Public. S'il a le bonheur de mériter son approbation, quoiqu'il y ait peu de gloire attachée au travail ingrat et fastidieux d'un Traducteur, je me déterminerai à donner les meilleurs ouvrages allemands, sur l'Histoire Naturelle, la Minéralogie, la Métallurgie et la Chymie. Tout le monde sait que l'Allemagne possede en ce genre des trésors qui ont été jusqu'ici comme enfouis pour la France.[1]

2. *Minéralogie ou Description générale du règne mineral par J. G. Wallerius* (Paris, Durand, 1753) followed by *Hydrologie* by the same author. Second edition, Paris,

---

[1] [The desire to make myself useful, with which every citizen should be animated, made me undertake the work I present to the public. If it has the good fortune to garner approval, although there is little glory attached to the tedious and thankless job of a translator, I will dedicate myselft to producing the best German books on natural history, mineralogy, metallurgy and chemistry. The world knows that Germany possesses treasures in this field that so far have been buried in France.]

Herrissant, 1759. Originally in Swedish (Wallerius was a professor of chemistry in the University of Upsala). German translation by J. D. Denso, Professor of Chemistry, Stargard, Pomerania. Holbach's translation was made from the German edition which Wallerius considered preferable to the Swedish. He was assisted by Bernard de Jussien and Rouelle, and the work was dedicated to a friend and co-worker in the natural sciences, Monsieur d'Arclais de Montamy.

3. *Introduction à la Minéralogie... oeuvre posthume de M. J. F. Henckel*, Paris, Cavelier, 1756, first published under title *Henckelius in Mineralogiâ redivivus*, Dresden, 1747, by his pupil, M. Stephani, as an outline of his lectures. Holbach's translation made from a German edition, corrected, with notes on new discoveries added.

4. *Chimie métallurgique... par M. C. Gellert*. Paris, Briasson, 1758, translated earlier. Approbation May 1, 1753, Privilege Dec. 21, 1754. Originally a text written by Gellert for four artillery officers whom the King of Sardinia sent to Freyburg to learn mining-engineering.

5. *Traités de physique, d'histoire naturelle, de mineralogy et de métallurgie*. Paris, Herrissant, 1759, by J. G. Lehmann, three vols. I. L'Art des Mines, II. Traité de la formation des métaux, III. Essai d'une histoire naturelle des couches de la terre. In his preface to the third volume Holbach has some interesting remarks about the deluge, the irony of which seems to have escaped the royal censor, Millet, *Docteur en Théologie*.

"La description si précise et si détaillée que Moïse fait du Deluge dans la Genèse, ayant une autorité infaillible, puis qu'elle n'est autre que celle de Dieu même, nous rend certains de la réalité et de l'universalité de ce châtiment terrible. Il s'agit simplement d'examiner si les naturalistes, tels que Woodward, Schenchzer, Buttner et M. Lehmann lui-même ne se sont points trompés, lorsqu'ils ont attribué à cet événement seul la formation des couches de la terre et lorsqu'ils s'en sont servis pour expliquer l'état actuel de notre globe. Il semble que rien ne doit nous empêcher d'agiter cette question; l'Ecriture sainte se contente de nous apprendre la voie miraculeuse dont Dieu s'est servi pour punir les crimes du genre humain; elle ne dit rien qui puisse limiter les sentiments des naturalistes sur les autres effets physiques que le déluge a pu produire. C'est une matière qu'elle paroît avoir abandonnée aux disputes des hommes." He then proceeds to question whether the deluge could have produced the results attributed to it and argues against catastrophism which, it must be remembered, was the received geological doctrine down to the days of Lyell. "Les causes les plus simples sont capables de produire au bout des siècles les effets les plus grands, surtout lorsqu'elles agissent incessament; et nous voyons toutes ces causes réunies agir perpétuellement sous nos yeux. Concluons, donc, de tout ce qui précède, que le déluge, seul et les feux souterrains seuls ne suffisent point pour expliquer la formation des couches de la terre. On risquera toujours de se tromper, lorsque par l'envie de simplifier on voudra dériver tous les phénomènes de la nature d'une seule et unique cause."[2]

---

[2] ["The so precise and so detailed description that Moses made of the Flood in Genesis, having infallible authority, then it is none other than God Himself who assures us of the reality and universality of this terrible punishment . We merely need to examine whether the naturalists, such as Woodward, Schenchzer, Buttner and Mr. Lehmann himself are wrong, when they attributed to this event solely the formation of the layers of the earth, which they have used to explain the current state of our globe. It seems that nothing should stop us from asking this question; the Scriptures are content to teach us of the miraculous event that God used to punish the crimes of mankind, it says nothing to limit naturalists' ideas about other physical effects that the flood could have produced. It is a matter that seems to have abandoned in the disputes of men. . . .The most simple causes can produce the biggest effects for centuries after, especially when acting incessantly, and we see all these combined causes acting perpetually before our eyes. Conclude, therefore, from all the above, that the flood alone, and subterranean fires alone are not sufficient to explain the formation of the layers of the earth. We always risk making mistakes when the urge to simplify leads us to derive all natural phenomena from a single cause."]

6. *Pyritologie* by J. F. Henkel, Paris, Herrissant, 1760, a large volume in quarto, translated by Holbach. It contains *Flora Saturnisans* (translated by M. Charas and reviewed by M. Roux), Henkel's *Opuscules Minéralogiques* and other treatises. Original editions: *Pyritologia*, Leipzig, 1725, 1754; *Flora Saturnisans*, Leipzig, 1721; *De Appropriatione Chymica*, Dresden, 1727, and *De Lapidum origine*, Dresden, 1734, translated into German, with excellent notes, Dresden, 1744, by M. C. F. Zimmermann, a pupil of M. Henkel. Holbach's translations seem to have been well received because he writes in this preface: "Je m'estimerai heureux si mon travail peut contribuer à entretenir et augmenter le goût universel qu'on a conçu pour le saine physique."

7. *Oeuvres métallurgiques* de M. J. C. Orschall, Paris, Hardy, 1760. Orschall still accepted the old alchemist tradition but was sound in practice and was the best authority on copper. Holbach does not attempt to justify his physics which was that of the preceding century. Orschall was held in high esteem by Henckel and Stahl.

8. *Recueil des mémoires des Académies d'Upsal et de Stockholm*, Paris, Didot, 1764. These records of experiments made in the Royal Laboratories of Sweden, founded in 1683 by Charles XI, had already been translated into German and English. Holbach's translation was made from the German and Latin. He promises further treatises on Agriculture, Natural History and Medicine.

9. *Traité du Soufre* by G. E. Stahl, Paris, Didot, 1766. In speaking of Stahl's theories Holbach says: "Il ne faut pas croire que ces connaissances soient des vérités stériles propres seulement à satisfaire une vaine curiosité, elles ont leur application aux travaux de la métallurgie qui leur doivent la

perfection où on les a portés depuis quelques temps."[3] Holbach understood very clearly the utility of science in his scheme of increasing the store of human well-being, and would doubtless have translated other useful works had not other interests prevented. There is a MSS. note of his in the Bibliothèque Nationale to M. Malesherbes, then Administrateur de la Librairie Royale; suggesting other German treatises that might well be translated. (MSS. 22194).

HOLBACH TO MALESHERBES

Monsieur

J'ai l'honneur de vous envoyer ci-joint la liste des ouvrages dont M. Liège fils pourrait entreprendre la traduction. Je n'en connais actuellement point d'autres qui méritent l'attention du public. M. Macquer m'a écrit une lettre qui a pour objet les mêmes choses dont vous m'avez fait l'honneur de me parler, et je lui fais la même réponse.

J'ai l'honneur d'être avec respect, Monsieur,

Votre très obéissant serviteur

D'HOLBACH

à Paris ce 6 d'avril 1761[4]

---

[3] [Do not believe that these facts are sterile truths suitable only to satisfy idle curiosity, they have their application to the work of metallurgy where they have been perfected over a long period of time.]

[4] [Sir, I have the honor to send herewith the list of books which Mr. Liege's son (*or* Mr Liege, Junior) could undertake to translate. I don't currently know of any others deserving public attention. Mr. Macquer has written me a letter about the same things that you have honored me by speaking of, and I have answered him in the same way.

I have the honor to be, with respect, Sir,

Your very obedient servant . . .]

The list of books was as follows:

1. Johann Kunckel's *Laboratorium Chymicum*, 8vo.
2. Georg Ernest Stahl's *Commentary on Becher's Metallurgy*, 8vo.
3. *Concordantia Chymica Becheri*, 40°, published by Stahl.
4. *Cadmologia*, or the *Natural History of Cobalt*, by J. G. Lehmann, Berlin, 1760, 4°.

After 1760 Holbach became interested in another line of intellectual activity, namely the writing and translation of anti-religious literature. His first book of this sort really appeared in 1761 although no copies bear this date. From 1767 on however he published a great many works of this character. It is convenient to deal first with his translations of English deistical writers. They are in chronological order.

1. *Esprit du clergé, ou le Christianisme primitif vengé des entreprises et des excès de nos Prêtres modernes*. Londres (Amsterdam), 1767. This book appeared in England in 1720 under the title of *The Independent Whig*; its author was Thomas Gordon (known through his Commentaries on Sallust and Tacitus) who wrote in collaboration with John Trenchard. The book was partially rewritten by Holbach and then touched up by Naigeon, who, according to a manuscript note by his brother, "atheised it as much as possible." It was sold with great secrecy and at a high price—a reward which the colporters demanded for the risk they ran in peddling seditious literature. The book was a violent attack on the spirit of domination which characterized the Christian priesthood at that time.

2. De L'imposture sacerdotale, ou Recueil de Pièces sur le clergé, Londres (Amsterdam), 1767. Another edition 1772 under title De la Monstruosité pontificale etc.

Contains translations of various pamphlets including Davisson, *A true picture of Popery*; Brown, *Popery a Craft*, London 1735; Gordon, *Apology for the danger of the church*, 1719; Gordon, *The Creed of an Independent Whig*, 1720.

3. Examen des Prophéties qui servent de fondement à la religion Chrétienne, Londres (Amsterdam), 1768. Translation of Anthony Collins, A Discourse on the Grounds and Reasons of the Christian Religion, London, 1724. Contains also The Scheme of literal Prophecy considered, 1727, also by Collins in answer to the works of Clarke, Sherlock, Chandler, Sykes, and especially to Whiston's Essay towards restoring the text of the Old Testament, one of the thirty-five works directed against Collins' original "Discourse". Copies of this work have become very rare.

4. *David, ou l'histoire de l'homme selon le coeur de Dieu.* Londres (Amsterdam), 1768. This work appeared in England in 1761 and is attributed to Peter Annet, also to John Noorthook. Some English eulogists of George II, Messrs. Chandler, Palmer and others, had likened their late King to David, "the man after God's own heart." The deists, struck by the absurdity of the comparison, proceeded to relate all the scandalous facts they could find recorded of David, and by clever distortions painted him as the most execrable of Kings, in a work entitled *David or the Man after God's Own Heart*, which formed the basis of Holbach's translation.

5. *Les prêtres démasqués ou des iniquités du clergé chrétien.* Londres, 1768. Translation of four discourses published under the title *The Ax laid to the root of Christian Priestcraft by a layman*, London, T. Cooper, 1742. A rare volume.

6. *Lettres philosophiques...* Londres (Amsterdam, 1768). Translation of J. Toland's *Letters to Serena*, London, 1704. The book, which had become very rare in Holbach's time, had caused a great scandal at the time of its publication and was much sought after by collectors. It contains five letters, the first three of which are by Toland, the other two and the preface by Holbach and Naigeon. The matters treated are, the origin of prejudices, the dogma of the immortality of the soul, idolatry, superstition, the system of Spinoza and the origin of movement in matter.

Diderot said of these works, in writing to Mlle. Volland Nov. 22, 1768 (*Oeuvres*, Vol. XVIII, p. 308): "Il pleut des bombes dans la maison du Seigneur. Je tremble toujours que quelqu'un de ces téméraires artilleurs-là ne s'en trouve mal. Ce sont les *Lettres philosophiques* traduites, ou supposées traduites, de l'anglais de Toland; c'est *l'Examen des prophéties*; c'est la *Vie de David ou de l'homme selon là coeur de Dieu*, ce sont mélle diables déchainés.—Ah! Madame de Blacy, je crains bien que le Fils de l'Homme ne soit à la porte; que la venue d'Elie ne soit proche, et que nous ne touchions au règne de l'Anti-christ. Tous les jours, quand je me lève, je regarde par ma fenêtre, si la grande prostituée de Babylone ne se promène point déjà dans les rues avec sa grande coupe à la main et s'il ne se fait aucun des signes prédits dans le firmament."[5]

7. *De la Cruauté religieuse*, Londres (Amsterdam). Considerations upon war, upon cruelty in general and religious cruelty in particular, London, printed for Thomas Hope, 1761.

8. *Dissertation critique sur les tourmens de l'enfer* printed in an original work, *L'Enfer détruit*, Londres (Amsterdam), 1769. A translation of Whitefoot's *The Torments of Hell*, the foundation and pillars thereof discover'd, search'd, shaken and remov'd. London, 1658.

9. In the *Recueil philosophique* edited by Naigeon, Londres (Amsterdam), 1770. I. Dissertation sur l'immortalité de l'âme. Translated from Hume. II. Dissertation sur le suicide (Hume).

---

[5] [It's raining bombs in the house of the Lord. I always tremble lest one of those brave artillerymen comes to harm. These are the *Philosophical Letters*, translated or supposedly translated, from the English of Toland, including *the Examination of Prophecies*, the *Life of David or The Man after God's Heart*, they are ? unchained devils. — Ah! Madame de Blacy, I fear that the Son of Man is not at the door, that the coming of Elijah is not close, and that we are not approaching the reign of the Antichrist. Every day when I wake I look out of my window to see if the Great Whore of Babylon is already walking in the streets with a great cup in her hand and if there are any of the foretold signs in the sky.]

III. Extrait d'un livre Anglais qui a pour titre le Christianisme aussi ancien que le monde. (Tindal, Christianity as old as Creation.)

10. *Esprit de Judaïsme, ou Examen raisonné de la Loi de Moyse*. Londres (Amsterdam), 1770 (1769), translated from Anthony Collins. With the exception of some of Holbach's own works this is one of the fiercest denunciations of Judaism and Christianity to be found in print. In fact, it is very much in the style of Holbach's anti-religious works and shows beyond a doubt that Holbach derived his inspiration from Collins and the more radical of the English school. The volume has become exceedingly rare.

After outlining the history of Judaism the book ends thus:

Ose, donc enfin, ô Europe! secouer le joug insupportable des préjugés qui t'affligent. Laisse à des Hébreux stupides, à des frénétiques imbéciles, à des Asiatiques lâches et dégradés, ces superstitions aussi avilissantes qu'insensées: elles ne sont point faites pour les habitans de ton climat. Occupe-toi du soin de perfectionner tes gouvernemens, de corriger tes lois, de réformer tes abus, de régler tes moeurs, et ferme pour toujours les yeux à ces vraies chimères, qui depuis tant de siècles n'ont servi qu'à retarder tes progrès vers la science véritable et à t'écarter de la route du bonheur.[6]

11. *Examen critique de la vie et des ouvrages de Saint Paul*, Londres (Amsterdam), 1770. A free translation of Peter Annet's *History and character of St. Paul examined*, written in answer to Lyttelton. New edition 1790 and translated back into English

---

[6] [Dare then, at last, O Europe! to shake off the intolerable yoke of the prejudices that afflict you. Leave to the stupid Hebrews, to the frantic fools, to the cowardly and degraded Asians, these debasing, senseless superstitions: they are not made for the inhabitants of your climate. Occupy yourself in perfecting your governments, correcting your laws, reforming abuses, regulating your morals, and close your eyes forever to these certain chimeras, which for so many centuries have only served to delay your progress toward real science and drive you away from the path of happiness.]

"from the French of Boulanger," London, R. Carlile, 1823. A rather unsympathetic account, but with flashes of real insight into "le système religieux des Chrétiens dont S. Paul fut évidemment le véritable architecte." (Epître dédicatoire.)

Annet said of Paul's type of man "l'enthousiaste s'enivre, pour l'ainsi dire, de son propre vin, il se persuade que la cause de ses passions est la cause de Dieu (p. 72), mais quelque violent qu'ait pu être l'enthousiasme de S. Paul, il sentait très bien que la doctrine qu'il prêchait devait paraître bizarre et insensée à des êtres raisonnables"[7] (p. 141).

12. *De la nature humaine, ou Exposition des facultés, des actions et des passions de l'âme*, Londres (Amsterdam), 1772. (Thomas Hobbes.) Reprinted in a French Edition of Hobbes' works by Holbach and Sorbière, 1787. Appeared first in English in 1640, omitted in a Latin Edition of Hobbes printed in Amsterdam. In spite of its brevity, Holbach considered this one of Hobbes' most important and luminous works.

13. *Discours sur les Miracles de Jesus Christ* (Amsterdam, 1780?). Translated from Woolston, whom Holbach admired very much for his uncompromising attitude toward truth. He suffered fines and imprisonments, but would not give up the privilege of writing as he pleased. The present discourse was the cause of a quarrel with his friend Whiston. He died Jan. 27, 1733, "avec beaucoup de fermeté... il se ferma les yeux et la bouche de ses propres mains, et rendit l'esprit."[8] This work exists in a manuscript book of 187 pages, written very fine, in the Bibliothèque Nationale (Mss. français 15224) and was current in France long before 1780. In fact it is mentioned by Grimm

---

[7] ["the enthusiast gets drunk, so to speak, on his own wine, he is convinced that the cause of his passions is the cause of God . . . but however violent the enthusiasm of St. Paul, he knew very well that the doctrine he preached would appear bizarre and insane to rational beings"]

[8] ["very firmly. . . he closed his eyes and mouth with his own hands, and gave up the ghost"]

before 1770, but the dictionaries (Barber, Quérard) generally date it from 1780.

Before turning to Holbach's original works mention should be made of a very interesting and extraordinary book that he brought to light, retouched, and later used as a kind of shield against the attacks of the parliaments upon his own works.

In 1766 he published a work *entitled L'Antiquité dévoilée par ses usages, ou Examen critique des principales Opinions, Cérémonies et Institutions religieuses et politiques des différens Peuples de la Terre*. Par feu M. Boulanger, Amsterdam, 1766. This is a work based on an original manuscript by Boulanger, who died in 1759, preceded by an excellent letter on him by Diderot, published also in the Gazette Littéraire.

The use made by Holbach of Boulanger's name makes it necessary to consider for a moment this almost forgotten writer. Nicholas Antoine Boulanger was born in 1722. As a child he showed so little aptitude for study that later his teachers could scarcely believe that he had turned out to be a really learned man. As Diderot observes, "ces exemples d'enfans, rendus ineptes entre les mains des Pédans qui les abrutissent en dépit de la nature la plus heureuse, ne sont pas rares, cependant ils surprennent toujours"[9] (p. 1). Boulanger studied mathematics and architecture, became an engineer and was employed by the government as inspector of bridges and highways. He passed a busy life in exacting outdoor work but at the same time his active intellect played over a large range of human interests. He became especially concerned with historical origins and set himself to learn Latin and Greek that he might get at the sources. Not satisfied that he had come to the root of the matter he learned Arabic, Syriac, Hebrew and Chaldean. Diderot says "Il lisait et étudiait partout, je l'ai moi-même rencontré sur les

[9] ["These examples of children, rendered inept at the hands of pedants who brutalize them despite the happiest of natures, are not uncommon, however, they always surprise"]

grandes routes avec un auteur rabinnique à la main."[10] He made a *mappemonde* in which the globe is divided in two hemispheres, one occupied by the continents, the other by the oceans, and by a singular coincidence he found that the meridian of the continental hemisphere passed through Paris. Some such rearrangement of hemispheres is one of the commonplaces of modern geography. He furnished such articles as, *Deluge, Corvée, Société* for the Encyclopedia and wrote several large and extremely learned books, among them *Recherches sur l'origine du Despotisme oriental* and *Antiquité dévoilée*. He died from overwork at the age of thirty-seven.

Boulanger's ideas on philosophy, mythology, anthropology and history are of extraordinary interest today. Diderot relates his saying—"Que si la philosophie avait trouvé tant d'obstacles parmi nous c'était qu'on avait commencé par où il aurait fallu finir, par des maximes abstraites, des raisonnemens généraux, des réflexions subtiles qui ont révolté par leur étrangeté et leur hardiesse et qu'on aurait admises sans peine si elles avaient été précédées de l'histoire des faits."[11] He carried over this inductive method into realm of history, which he thought had been approached from the wrong side, i.e., the metaphysical, "par consulter les lumières de la raison"[12] (p. 8). He continues, "j'ai pensé qu'il devait y avoir quelques circonstances *particulières*. Un fait et non une spéculation métaphysique m'a toujours

---

[10] ["He read and studied everywhere, I myself met him on the highways with a rabbinical author in hand."]

[11] ["That if philosophy had found so many obstacles among us, so that we started where we should have finished, with abstract maxims, generalizations, subtle reflections which were shocking in their strangeness and daring, that one would have admitted without difficulty it they had been preceded with factual history."]

[12] ["by consulting the light of reason"]

semblé devoir être et tribut naturel et nécessaire de l'histoire."[13] Curiously enough the central fact in history appeared to Boulanger to be the deluge, and on the basis of it he attempted to interpret the *Kulturgeschichte* of humanity. It is a bit unfortunate that he took the deluge quite as literally as he did; his idea, however, is obviously the influence of environmental pressure on the changing beliefs and practices of mankind. Under the spell of this new point of view, he writes, "Ce qu'on appelle l'histoire n'en est que la partie la plus ingrate, la plus uniforme, la plus inutile, quoi qu'elle soit la plus connue. La véritable histoire est couverte par le voile des temps"[14] (p. 7). Boulanger however was not to be daunted and on the firm foundation of the fact of some ancient and universal catastrophe, as recorded on the surface of the earth and in human mythology, he proceeds to inquire into the moral effects of the changes in the physical environment back to which if possible the history of antiquity must be traced. Man's defeat in his struggle with the elements made him religious, *hinc prima mali labes*. "Son premier pas fut un faux pas, sa première maxime fut une erreur"[15] (p. 4 sq). But it was not his fault nor has time repaired the evil moral effects of that early catastrophe. "Les grandes révolutions physiques de notre globe sont les véritables époques de l'histoire des nations"[16] (p. 9). Hence have arisen the various psychological states through which mankind has passed. Contemporary savages are still in the primitive state—Boulanger properly emphasizes the relation of anthropology to history—"On

[13] ["I thought there must be some special circumstances. A fact, rather than a metaphysical speculation, has always seemed to me to be absolute and natural tribute(?) and historical necessity."]

[14] ["What we call history is only the most thankless, most uniform, most useless part, whatever is the best known. Real history is covered by the veil of time."]

[15] ["His first step was a misstep, his first maxim was a mistake"]

[16] ["The great physical revolutions of our world are the real epochs in the history of nations"]

aperçoit qu'il y a une nouvelle manière de voir et d'écrire l'histoire des hommes"[17] (p. 12) and with a vast store of anthropological and folklorist learning he writes it so that his assailant, Fabry d'Autrey, in his *Antiquité justifiée* (Paris, 1766) is obliged to say with truth, "Ce n'est point ici un tissus de mensonges grossiers, de sophismes rebattus et bouffons, appliqués d'un air méprisant aux objets les plus intéressants pour l'humanité. C'est une enterprise sérieuse et réfléchie"[18] (p. 11).

In 1767 Holbach published his first original work, a few copies of which had been printed in Nancy in 1761. This work was *Le Christianisme dévoilé ou Examen des principes et des effets de la religion Chrétienne*. Par feu M. Boulanger. Londres (Amsterdam), 1767. There were several other editions the same year, one printed at John Wilkes' private press in Westminster. It was reprinted in later collections of Boulanger's works, and went through several English and Spanish editions. The form of the title and the attribution of the work to Boulanger were designed to set persecution on the wrong track. There has been some discussion as to its authorship. Voltaire and Laharpe attributed it to Damilaville, at whose book shop it was said to have been sold, but M. Barbier has published detailed information given him by Naigeon to the effect that Holbach entrusted his manuscript to M. De Saint-Lambert, who had it printed by Leclerc at Nancy in 1761. Most of the copies that got to Paris at that time were bought by several officers of the King's regiment then in garrison at Nancy, among them M. de Villevielle, a friend of Voltaire and of Condorcet. Damilaville did not sell a single copy and even had a great deal of trouble to get one for Holbach who waited for it a long time. This circumstantial evidence is of greater value than the statement of

[17] ["We realise that there is a new way of seeing and writing the history of mankind"]

[18] ["There is no tissue of crude lies here, no trite, buffoonish sophistries, applied contemptuously to the objects of mankind's greatest interest. This is a serious and thoughtful enterprise"]

Voltaire who was in the habit of attributing anonymous works to whomever he pleased.[19]

The edition of 1767 was printed in Amsterdam as were most of Holbach's works. We have the details of their publication from Naigeon *cadet*, a copyist, whose brother, J. A. Naigeon, was Holbach's literary factotum. In a manuscript note in his copy of the *Système de la Nature* he tells how he copied nearly all Holbach's works, either at Paris or at Sedan, where he was stationed, and where his friend Blon, the postmaster, aided him, passing the manuscripts on to a Madame Loncin in Liège, who in turn was a correspondent of Marc-Michel Rey, the printer in Amsterdam. Sometimes they were sent directly by the diligence or through travellers. This account agrees perfectly with information given M. Barbier orally by Naigeon *aîné*. After being printed in Holland the books were smuggled into France *sous le manteau*, as the expression is, and sold at absurd rates by colporters.[20]

Diderot writing to Falconet early in 1768[21] says: "Il pleut des livres incrédules. C'est un feu roulant qui crible le sanctuaire de toutes parts... L'intolérance du gouvernment s'accroit de jour en jour. On dirait que c'est un projet formé d'éteindre ici les lettres, de ruiner le commerce de librairie et de nous réduire à la besace et à la stupidité... *Le Christianisme dévoilé* s'est vendu jusqu'à quatre louis."[22]

When caught the colporters were severely punished. Diderot gives the following instance in a letter to Mlle. Volland Oct. 8,

---

[19] Barbier, *Dict.*, Vol. I, p. 175 sq.

[20] Barbier, Vol. I, p. xxxiii, note.

[21] *Oeuvres*, Vol. XVIII, p. 265.

[22] ["It's raining sceptical books. It's a wildfire penetrating the sanctuary from all sides . . . The Government's intolerance is increasing daily. It looks like a project designed to extinguish writing here, ruining the bookselling business and reducing us to beggary and stupidity . . . *Christianity Unveiled* is being sold for up to four pounds."]

1768 (Avézac-Lavigne, *Diderot*, p. 161): "Un apprenti avait reçu, en payment ou autrement, d'un colporteur appelé Lécuyer, deux exemplaires du *Christianisme dévoilé* et il avait vendu un de ces exemplaires à son patron. Celui-ci le défère au lieutenant de police. Le colporteur, sa femme et l'apprenti sont arrêtés tous les trois; ils viennent d'être piloriés, fouettés et marqués, et l'apprenti condamné à neuf ans de galères, le colporteur à cinq ans, et la femme à l'hôpital pour toute sa vie."[23]

There are two very interesting pieces of contemporary criticism of *Le Christianisme dévoilé*, one by Voltaire, the other by Grimm. Voltaire writes in a letter to Madame de Saint Julien December 15, 1766 (*Oeuvres*, XLIV, p. 534, ed. Garnier): "Vous m'apprenez que, dans votre société, on m'attribue *Le Christianisme dévoilé* par feu M. Boulanger, mais je vous assure que les gens au fait ne m'attribuent point du tout cet ouvrage. J'avoue avec vous qu'il y a de la clarté, de la chaleur, et quelque fois de l'éloquence; mais il est plein de répétitions, de négligences, de fautes contre la langue et je serais très-fâché de l'avoir fait, non seulement comme académicien, mais comme philosophe, et encore plus comme citoyen.

"Il est entièrement opposé à mes principes. Ce livre conduit à l'athéisme que je déteste. J'ai toujours regardé l'athéisme comme le plus grand égarement de la raison, parce qu'il est aussi ridicule de dire que l'arrangement du monde ne prouve pas un artisan suprême qu'il serait impertinent de dire qu'une horloge ne prouve pas un horloger.

"Je ne réprouve pas moins ce livre comme citoyen; l'auteur paraît trop ennemi des puissances. Des hommes qui penseraient comme lui ne formeraient qu'une anarchie: et je vois trop, par

---

[23] ["An apprentice had received, as payment or otherwise, from a hawker named Lecuyer, two copies of *Christianity Unveiled* and he had sold one of these copies to his boss. The latter notifies a police lieutenant. The hawker, his wife and the apprentice are all three arrested and pilloried, whipped and branded, with the apprentice condemned to nine years in the galleys, the hawker to five years, and the wife to the workhouse for life."]

l'example de Genève, combien l'anarchie est à craindre. Ma coutume est d'écrire sur la marge de mes livres ce que je pense d'eux, vous verrez, quand vous daignerez venir à Ferney, les marges de *Christianisme dévoilé* chargés de remarques qui montrent que l'auteur s'est trompé sur les faits les plus essentiels."[24] These notes may be read in Voltaire's works (Vol. XXXI, p. 129, ed. Garnier) and the original copy of *Le Christianisme dévoilé* in which he wrote them is in the British Museum (c 28, k 3) where it is jealously guarded as one of the most precious autographs of the Patriarch of Ferney.

Grimm's notice is from the *Correspondance Littéraire* of August 15, 1763 (Vol. V, p. 367). "Il existe un livre intitulé *le Christianisme dévoilé ou Examen des principes et des effets de la religion Chrétienne*, par feu M. Boulanger, volume in 8°. On voit d'abord qu'on lui a donné ce titre pour en faire le pendant de *l'Antiquité dévoilée*; mais il ne faut pas beaucoup se connaître en manière pour sentir que ces deux ouvrages ne sont pas sortis de la même plume. On peut assurer avec la même certitude que celui dont nous parlons ne vient point de la fabrique de Ferney,

---

[24] ["You tell me that in your social circle, people ascribe *Christianity Unveiled* by the late M. Boulanger to me, but I assure you that people don't attribute this work to me at all. I confess to you that there is clarity, warmth, and occasional eloquence, but it is full of repetitions, omissions, and sins against language and I would be very sorry to have written it, not only as an academician, but as a philosopher, and even more as a citizen.

"It is entirely opposed to my principles. This book leads to atheism which I hate. I have always considered atheism to be the greatest aberration of reason, because it is ridiculous to say that the arrangement of the world does not prove a supreme craftsman as it would be impertinent to say that a clock does not prove a watchmaker.

"I condemn this book just as much as a citizen, the author seems too anti the powers that be. Men who think like him would form an anarchy: and I see too, by the Geneva example, how anarchy is to be feared. My custom is to write on the margins of my books what I think of them, you will see, when you condescend to come to Ferney, the margins of *Christianity Unveiled* full of remarks that show that the author was mistaken about the most essential facts."]

parce que j'aimerais mieux croire que le patriache eût pris la lune avec ses dents; cela serait moins impossible que de guetter sa manière et son allure si complètement qu'il n'en restât aucune trace quelconque. Par la même raison, je ne crois ce livre d'aucun de nos philosophes connus, parce que je n'y trouve la manière d'aucun de ceux qui ont écrit. D'òu vient-il donc? Ma foi, je serais fâché de le savoir, et je crois que l'auteur aura sagement fait de ne mettre personne dans son secret. C'est le livre le plus hardi et le plus terrible qui ait jamais parti dans aucun lieu du monde. La préface consiste dans une lettre où l'auteur examine si la réligion est reéllement nécessaire ou seulement utile au maintien ou à la police des empires, et s'il convient de la respecter sous ce point de vue. Comme il établit la négative, il entreprend en conséquence de prouver, par son ouvrage, l'absurdité et l'incohérence du dogme Chrétien et de la mythologie qui en résulte, et l'influence de cette absurdité sur les têtes et sur les âmes. Dans la seconde partie, il examine la morale chrétienne, et il prétend prouver que dans ses principes généraux elle n'a aucun avantage sur toutes les morales du monde, parce que la justice et la bonté sont recommandées dans tous les catéchismes de l'univers, et que chez aucun peuple, quelque barbare qu'il fut, on n'a jamais enseigné qu'il fallût être injuste et méchant. Quant à ce que la morale chrétienne a de particulier, l'auteur pretend démontrer qu'elle ne peut convenir qu'à des enthousiastes peu propres aux devoirs de la société, pour lesquels les hommes sont dans ce monde. Il entreprend de prouver, dans la troisième partie, que la religion chrétienne a eu les effets politiques les plus sinistres et les plus funestes, et que le genre humain lui doit tous les malheurs dont il a été accablé depuis quinze à dix-huit siècles, sans qu'on en puisse encore prévoir la fin.

Ce livre est écrit avec plus de véhémence que de véritable éloquence; il entraine. Son style est châtié et correct, quoique un peu dur et sec; son ton est grave et soutenu. On n'y apprend rien de nouveau, et cependant il attache et intéresse. Malgré son incroyable témérité, on ne peut refuser à l'auteur la qualité d'homme de bien fortement épris du bonheur de sa race et de la prospérité des sociétés; mais je pense que ses bonnes intentions seraient une sauvegarde bien faible contre les mandements et les réquisitions."[25] This is a clear and fair account of a book that is

---

[25] [There is a book called *Christianity Unveiled or Examination of the principles and effects of the Christian religion*, by the late M. Boulanger, in octavo form. First we see that it was given this title as counterpoise to *The Ancient World Unveiled*, but it does not take much familiarity with the style to see that these two books are not from the same pen. We can say with the same certainty that this thing we are talking about does not come from the Ferney factory, because it would be easier to believe that the patriarch had taken a bite out of the moon, it would be less impossible than for him to have altered his manner and style so completely that no trace remained at all. For the same reason I don't believe this book is by any of our well-known philosophers, because I do not detect the style of any that are in print. Where does he come from? Good lord, I should be sorry to know, and I think the author has wisely not entrusted anyone with his secret. This book is the boldest and most terrible that has ever appeared anywhere in the world. The preface consists of a letter in which the author asks whether religion is really necessary or only useful in policing empires, and whether it is advisable to respect it for that reason. As he answers in the negative, he begins accordingly to prove, in his work, the absurdity and inconsistency of Christian dogma and the resulting mythology, and the effects of this nonsense on minds and souls. In the second part he examines Christian morality, and claims to prove that in its general principles it has no advantage over all the moral systems of the world, because justice and goodness are recommended in every catechism in the universe and in those of every race, however barbarous they appear, and no one was ever taught that they ought to be unjust and wicked. As for Christian morality in particular, the author claims to show that it is only suitable for enthusiasts little suited to the duties of society, for such men are in this world. He undertakes to prove, in the third part, that the Christian religion has had the most sinister and deadly political effects, and that mankind owes it all the bad things that have happened in the last fifteen to eighteen centuries, with no end in sight.

This book is written with more vehemence than real eloquence: it leads. The style is chaste and correct, if somewhat hard and dry, and the tone is serious and sustained. We do not learn anything new, and yet it grabs our interest. Despite his incredible rashness, one cannot deny that the author has the mark of a good man greatly devoted to the happiness of his race and to the prospering of society; but I think his good intentions would be a very feeble defense against the commandments and requisitions.]

without doubt the severest criticism of the theory and practice of historical Christianity ever put in print.

The church very naturally did not let such a book pass unanswered. Abbé Bergier, a heavy person, triumphantly refuted Holbach in eight hundred pages in his *Apologia de la Religion Chrétienne contre l'Auteur du Christianisme dévoilé*, Paris, 1769, which finishes with the fatal prophecy, "Nous avons de surs garans de nos espérances: tant que le sang auguste de S. Louis sera sur le trône, *il n'y a point de révolutions à craindre ni dans la Religion ni dans la politique*. La religion Chrétienne fondée sur la parole de Dieu... triomphera des nouveaux Philosophes. Dieu qui veille sur son ouvrage n'a pas besoin de nos faibles mains pour le soutenir"[26] (Psaume 32, vs. 10, 11).

2. There already existed in 1767 another work by Holbach entitled *Théologie portative ou Dictionnaire Abrégé de la Religion Chrétienne. Par Mr Abbé Bernier*. Londres (Amsterdam), 1768 (1767). This book went through many editions and was augmented by subsequent authors and editors. Voltaire was already writing to d'Alembert about it August 14, 1767.[27]

In a letter to Damilaville, October 16, he writes (Vol. XIV, p. 406):

Depuis trois mois il y a une douzaine d'ouvrages d'une liberté extrême, imprimés en Hollande. *La Théologie portative* n'est nullement théologique: ce n'est qu'une plaisanterie continuelle par ordre alphabétique; mais il faut avouer qu'il y a des traits si comiques que plusieurs théologiens mêmes ne pourront s'empêcher d'en rire. Les jeunes gens et les femmes

---

[26] ["We have sure pledges of our hopes, as long as the august blood of St. Louis is on the throne, *we fear no revolutions in either religion or politics*. The Christian religion, based on the word of God, . . . will triumph over the new philosophers. God, who watches over his creation, does not need our feeble hands to defend him."]

[27] *Oeuvres*, Vol. XIV, p. 352.

lisent cette folie avec avidité. Les éditions de tous les livres dans ce goût se multiplient.[28]

And on February 8, 1768, he wrote:

On fait tous les jours des livres contre la religion, dont je voudrais bien imiter le style pour la défendre. Y a-t-il de plus salé, que la plupart des traits qui se trouvent dans la *Théologie portative*? Y a-t-il rien de plus vigoreux, de plus profondément raisonné, d'écrit avec une éloquence plus audacieuse et plus terrible, que le *Militaire philosophe*, ouvrage qui court toute l'Europe? [by Naigeon and Holbach] Lisez la *Théologie portative*, et vous ne pourrez vous empêcher de rire, en condammant la coupable hardiesse de l'auteur. Lisez *l'Imposture sacerdotale*—vous y verrez le style de Démosthène. Ces livres malheuresement inondent l'Europe; mais quelle est la cause de cette inondation? Il n'y en a point d'autre que les querelles théologiques qui ont révolté les laïques. *Il s'est fait une révolution dans l'esprit humain que rien ne peut plus arrêter: les persécutions ne pourraient qu'irriter le mal.*[29]

---

[28] [In the last three months there have been a dozen books taking extreme liberties, printed in Holland. *Portable Theology* is not theological: it's just an ongoing joke in alphabetical order, but we must admit that some of its features are so comical that several theologians cannot stop themselves laughing. Young men and women avidly read this nonsense. Editions of all these kinds of books are multiplying.]

[29] The italics are mine [the author's].

[Every day there are books against religion, whose style I would like to imitate in defense. Is there anything more exaggerated than most of the features found in the *Portable Theology*? Is there anything more vigorous, more deeply reasoned, written with a bolder and more terrible eloquence than in the *Military Philosopher*, a work that is overrunning Europe? . . . Read the *Portable Theology*, and you cannot stop yourself laughing, whilst condemning the culpable boldness of the author. Read the *Priestly Imposture* — you will see the style of Demosthenes. Unfortunately these books are flooding Europe, but what is the cause of the flood? It is none other than the theological disputes which have shocked the laity. *A revolution has been incited in the human spirit that nothing can stop any more: persecution will only stir up more evil.*]

It is to be noted however that Voltaire's sentiments varied according to the point of view of the person to whom he was writing. In a letter to d'Alembert, May 24, 1769 (Vol. LXV, p. 453), he calls the *Théologie portative* "un ouvrage à mon gré, très plaisant, auquel je n'ai assurément nulle part, ouvrage que je serais très fâché d'avoir fait, et que je voudrais bien avoir été capable de faire."[30] But in a letter to the Bishop of Annecy June, 1769, he writes (Vol. XXVIII, p. 73): "Vous lui [M. de Saint Florentin] imputez, à ce que je vois par vos lettres, des livres misérables, et jusqu'à *la Theologie portative*, ouvrage fait apparemment dans quelque cabaret; vous n'êtes pas obligé d'avoir du goût, mais vous êtes obligé d'être juste"[31] (Vol. XXVIII, p. 73). Diderot even said of the book: "C'est un assez bon nombre de bonnes plaisanteries noyées dans un beaucoup plus grand nombre de mauvaises"[32] and this criticism is just. A few examples of the better jokes will suffice:

Adam: C'est le premier homme, Dieu en fait un grand nigaud, qui pour complaire à sa femme eut la bêtise de mordre dans une pomme que ses descendans n'ont point encore pu digérer.

Idées Innées: Notions inspirées des Prêtres de si bonne heure, si souvent répétées, que devenu grand l'on croît les avoir eu toujours ou les avoir reçus dès le ventre de sa mère.

Jonas: La baleine fut à la fin obligée de le vomir tant un Prophète est un morceau difficile à digérer.

---

[30] ["a book which is, in my opinion, very amusing, in which I assuredly had no part, a book that I would be very keen to have written, and I do wish I were capable of writing it."]

[31] ["You impute to him [M. de Saint Florentin], from what I see in your letters, some wretched books, even the *Portable Theology*, a work apparently written in some tavern; you don't have to have good taste, but you should be fair"]

[32] ["There's quite a few good jokes drowned in a much larger number of bad ones."]

Magie: Il y en a de deux sortes, la blanche et la noire. La première est très sainte et se pratique journellement dans l'église.

Protestants: Chrétiens amphibies.

Vierge: C'est la mère du fils de Dieu et belle-mère de l'église.

Visions: Lanternes magiques que de tout temps le Père Eternel s'est amusé à montrer aux Saintes et aux Prophètes.[33]

3. Holbach furnished the last chapter of Naigeon's book *Le Militaire philosophe, ou Difficulties sur la religion*, Londres (Amsterdam), 1768. Voltaire ascribed the work to St. Hyacinthe. Grimm recognized that the last chapter was by another hand and considered it the weakest part of the book. It attempts to demonstrate that all supernatural religions have been harmful to society and that the only useful religion is natural religion or morals. The book was refuted by Guidi, in a "*Lettre a M. le Chevalier de... [Barthe] entraîné dans l'irreligion par un libelle intitulé Le Militaire philosophe* (1770, 12mo).

4. Holbach's next book was *La Contagion sacrée ou l'Histoire naturelle de la Superstition*, Londres (Amsterdam),

---

[33] [Adam: The first man, God makes him a great simpleton, who to please his wife stupidly bites into an apple that his descendants haven't yet managed to digest.

Innate ideas: Notions dreamt up by Priests off the cuff, but so often repeated that the belief grows that they've always been around, or were implanted in the womb.

Jonah: The whale eventually had to vomit as a Prophet is rather difficult to digest.

Magic: There are two kinds, white and black. The first is very holy and is practiced daily in church.

Protestants: Amphibian Christians.

Virgin: The mother of the son of God and stepmother of the church.

Visions: Magic lanterns that the Eternal Father often amuses himself by showing to Saints and Prophets.]

1768. In his preface Holbach attributed the alleged English original of this work to John Trenchard but that was only a ruse to avoid persecution. The book is by Holbach. It has gone through many editions and been translated into English and Spanish. The first edition had an introduction by Naigeon. According to him manuscripts of this book became quite rare at one time and were supposed to have been lost. Later they became more common and this edition was corrected by collation with six others.

[34]The letters were written in 1764, according to Lequinio (*Feuilles posthumes*), who had his information from Naigeon, to Marguerite, Marchioness de Vermandois in answer to a very touching and pitiful letter from that lady who was in great trouble over religion. Her young husband was a great friend of the Holbachs, but having had a strict Catholic bringing up she was shocked at their infidelity and warned by her confessor to keep away from them. "Yet in their home she saw all the domestic virtues exemplified and beheld that sweet and unchangeable affection for which the d'Holbachs were eminently distinguished among their acquaintances and which was remarkable for its striking contrast with the courtly and Christian habits of the day. Her natural good sense and love for her friends struggled with her monastic education and reverence for the priests. The conflict rendered her miserable and she returned to her country seat to brood over it. In this state of mind she at length wrote to the Baron and laid open her situation requesting him to comfort, console, and enlighten her."[35] His letters accomplished the desired effect and he later published them in the hope that they would do as much for others. They were carefully revised before they were sent to the press. All the purely personal passages were omitted and others added to hide

---

[34] [Editor's note: at this point there appears to be some text omitted from the published edition. A sentence introducing the fifth book in this list, "Letters to Eugenie", has been lost.]

[35] Middleton's translation, preface.

the identity of the persons concerned. Letters of the sort to religious ladies were common at this time. Fréret's were preventive, Holbach's curative, but appear to be rather strong dose for a *dévote*. Other examples are Voltaire's *Epître à Uranie* and Diderot's *Entretien d'un Philosophe avec la Maréchale de....*

6. In 1769 Holbach published two short treatises on the doctrine of eternal punishment which claimed to be translations from English, but the originals are not to be found. The titles are *De l'intolérance convaincue de crime et de folie* as it is sometimes given, and—

7. *L'Enfer détruit ou Examen raisonné du Dogme de l'Eternité des Peines*. Londres, Amsterdam, 1769. This letter was translated into English under the title *Hell Destroyed!* "Now first translated from the French of d'Alembert without any mutilations," London 1823, which led Mr. J. Hibbert to say, "I know not why English publishers attribute this awfully sounding work to the cautious, not to say timid d'Alembert. It was followed by Whitefoot's *'Torments of Hell,'* now first translated from the French."[36]

Of Holbach's remaining works on religion two, *Histoire critique de Jésus Christ* and *Tableau des Saints*, date from 1770 when he began to publish his more philosophical works.

8. The *Histoire critique de Jésus Christ ou Analyse raisonnée des Evangiles* was published without name of place or date. It was preceded by Voltaire's *Epître à Uranie*. It is an extremely careful but unsympathetic analysis of the Gospel accounts, emphasizing all the inconsistencies and interpreting them with a literalness that they can ill sustain. From this rationalistic view-point Holbach found the Gospels a tissue of absurdities and contradictions. His method, however, would not be followed by the critique of today.

---

[36] Cf. p. 106. [Bibliography Part I]

9. The *Tableau des Saints* is a still more severe criticism of the heroes of Christendom. Holbach's proposition is "La raison ne connaît qu'une mesure pour juger et les hommes et les choses, c'est l'utilité réelle et permanente, qui en résulte pour notre espèce,"[37] (p. 111). Judged by this standard, the saints with their eyes fixed on another world have fallen far short. "Ils se flattèrent de mériter le ciel en se rendant parfaitement inutile à la terre"[38] (p. xviii). Holbach much prefers the heroes of classical antiquity. The book is violent but learned throughout, and deals not only with the Jewish patriarchs from Moses on but with the church fathers and Christian Princes down to the contemporary defenders of the faith. After a rather one-sided account of the most dreary characters and events in Christian history, Holbach concludes: "Tel fut, tel est, et tel sera toujours l'esprit du Christianisme: il est aisé de sentir qu'il est incompatible avec les principes les plus évidens de la morale et de la saine politique"[39] (p. 208).

10. In *Recueil philosophique*, Londres (Amsterdam), 1770, edited by Naigeon. Réflexions sur les craintes de la Mort. Problème important—La Religion est-elle nécessaire à la morale et utile à la Politique. Par M. Mirabaud.

11. *Essai sur les préjugés, ou De l'influence des opinions sur les moeurs et sur le bonheur des Hommes*. Londres (Amsterdam), 1770, under name of Dumarsais. The book pretended to be an elaboration of Dumarsais' essay on the *Philosophe* published in the *Nouvelles libertés de penser*, 1750.

---

[37] ["Reason knows only one measure for judging both men and things; it is of real and permanent use, and gave rise to our species"]

[38] ["They flattered themselves that they merited heaven by making themselves perfectly useless on earth"]

[39] ["This was, is, and will always be the spirit of Christianity: it is easy to feel that it is incompatible with the most outstanding principles of morality and sound policy"]

The special interest connected with it was the refutation Frederick the Great published under the title *Examen de l'Essai sur les préjugés*, Londres, Nourse, 1770 (16 mo). The King of Prussia writing from the point of view of a practical, enlightened despot, took special exception to Holbach's remarks on government. "Il l'outrage avec autant de grossièreté que d'indécence, il force le gouvernement de prendre fait et cause avec l'église pour s'opposer à l'ennemi commun. Mais, quand avec un acharnement violent et les traits de la plus âcre satire, il calomnie son Roi et le gouvernement de son pays, on le prend pour un frénétique echappé de ses chaînes, et livré aux transports les plus violens de sa rage. Quoi, Monsieur le philosophe, protecteur des moeurs et de la vertu, ignorez vous qu'un bon citoyen doit respecter la forme de gouvernement sous laquelle il vit, ignorez vous qu'il ne convient point à un particulier d'insulter les Puissances..." (p. 28).

"Non content d'insulter à toutes les têtes couronnés de l'Europe, notre philosophe s'amuse, en passant, à répandre du ridicule sur les ouvrages de Hugo Grotius. J'oserais croire qu'il n'en sera pas cru sur sa parole, et que le *Droit de la guerre et de la paix* ira plus loin à la postérité que *l'Essai sur les préjugés*" (p. 39).[40]

---

[40] ["He offends with contempt as well as rudeness, he forces the government to take up the cause with the church to oppose the common enemy. But when with violent obstinacy and characteristics of the bitterest satire, he slanders his King and his Government, we take him for a lunatic escaped from his chains, and delivered to the most violent transports of his rage. Mr. Philosopher, protector of morals and virtue, are you unaware that a good citizen should respect the form of government under which he lives, don't you know it's inappropriate to insult the Powers that be.. .?

Not content with insulting all the crowned heads of Europe, our philosopher amuses himself, in passing, by ridiculing the works of Hugo Grotius. I dare to believe that he will not be taken at his word, and *On the Law of War and Peace* will last longer in posterity than the *Essay on Prejudice*".]

Holbach in his anti-militaristic enthusiasm had used the words "bourreaux mercenaires"; "epithète élégante," continues Frederick, "dont il honore les guerriers. Mais souffrions nous qu'un cerveau brûlé insulte au plus noble emploi de la Societé?" (p.49). He goes on to defend war in good old-fashioned terms. "Vous déclamez contre la guerre, elle est funeste en elle-même; mais c'est un mal comme ces autres fléaux du ciel qu'il faut supposer nécessaires dans l'arrangement de cet univers parce qu'ils arrivent périodiquement et qu'aucun siècle n'a pu jusqu'à présent d'en avoir été exempt. J'ai prouvé que de tout temps l'erreur a dominé dans ce monde; et comme une chose aussi constante peut être envisagée comme une loi général de la nature, j'en conclus que ce qui a été toujours sera toujours le même"[41] (p. 19).

Frederick sent his little refutation to Voltaire for his compliments which were forthcoming. A few days after Voltaire wrote to d'Alembert:

Le roi de Prusse vous a envoyé, sans doute, son petit écrit contre un livre imprimé cette année, intitulé *Essai sur les préjugés*, ce roi a aussi les siens, qu'il faut lui pardonner; on n'est pas roi pour rien. Mais je voudrais savoir quel est l'auteur de cet *Essai* contre lequel sa majesté prussienne s'amuse à écrire un peu durement. Serait-il de Diderot? serait-il de Damilaville?

---

[41] ["mercenary executioners . . . an elegant epithet, . . . which honors warriors. But should we suffer a brain-burning insult against society's noblest work? . . . You declaim against war, that is fatal in itself; it is an evil just like the other scourges of heaven in that it must be supposed necessary in the arrangement of the universe because wars happen regularly and so far, no century has managed to be free of them. I proved that, historically, wrongdoing has always dominated this world, and as something so constant can be seen as a general law of nature, I conclude that what has been will always be."]

serait-il d'Helvetius? peut-être ne le connaissez-vous point, je le crois imprimé en Hollande[42] (Vol. LXVI, p. 304).

D'Alembert answered:

Oui, le roi de Prusse m'a envoyé son écrit contre *l'Essai sur les préjugés*. Je ne suis point étonné que ce prince n'ait pas goûté l'ouvrage; je l'ai lu depuis cette réfutation et il m'a paru bien long, bien monotone et trop amer. Il me semble que ce qu'il y de bon dans ce livre aurait pu et dû être noyé dans moins de pages et je vois que vous en avez porté à peu près le même jugement[43] (Vol. LXVI, p. 324).

In spite of these unfavorable judgments the *Essai* was reprinted as late as 1886 by the Bibliotheque Nationale in its *Collection des meilleurs auteurs anciens et modernes*, still attributed to Dumarsais with the account of his life by "le citoyen Daube" which graced the edition of the year I. (1792)

12. Early in 1770 appeared Holbach's most famous book, the *Système de la Nature*, the only book that is connected with his name in the minds of most historians and philosophers. It seems wiser, however, to deal with this work in a chapter apart and continue the account of his later publications.

13. The next of which was *Le bon-sens, ou idées naturelles opposées aux idées surnaturelles. Par l'Auteur du Système de la Nature*, Londres (Amsterdam), 1772. This work has gone

---

[42] ["The King of Prussia has sent you, no doubt, his little piece against a book printed this year, entitled *Essay on Prejudice*, the king has his own (prejudices) too, he should forgive him; he isn't king for nothing. But I want to know who the author of this essay is, against which his Prussian majesty likes to write a little severely. Is it Diderot? Is it Damilaville? Is it Helvetius? Perhaps you haven't seen it, I believe it was printed in Holland."]

[43] ["Yes, the King of Prussia sent me his piece against the *Essay on Prejudice*. I am not surprised that the book was not to the prince's taste; from what I read in his refutation it seemed very long, very monotonous and too bitter. I think that what good there is in this book could and should have been embedded in fewer pages, and I see that you have reached close to the same opinion."]

through twenty-five editions or more and has been translated into English, German, Italian and Spanish. As early as 1791 it began to be published under the name of the curé Jean Meslier d'Etrépigny, made so famous by Voltaire's publication of what was supposed to be his last will and testament in which on his death bed he abjured and cursed Christianity. Some editions contain in the preface Letters by Voltaire and his sketch of Jean Meslier. The last reprint was by De Laurence, Scott & Co., Chicago, 1910. The book is nothing more or less than the *Système de la Nature*, in a greatly reduced and more readable form.

Voltaire, to whom it was attributed by some, said to d'Alembert, "Il y a plus que du bon sens dans ce livre, il est terrible. S'il sort de la boutique du *Système de la Nature*, l'auteur s'est bien perfectionné." D'Alembert answered: "Je pense comme vous sur le *Bon-sens* qui me paraît un bien plus terrible livre que le *Système de la Nature*."[44] These remarks were inscribed by Thomas Jefferson on the title page of his copy of *Bon-sens*. The book has gone through several editions in the United States and was sold at a popular price. The German translation was published in Baltimore on the basis of a copy found in a second-hand book store in New Orleans. The most serious work written against it is a long and carefully written treatise against materialism by an Italian monk, Gardini, entitled *L'anima umana e sue proprietà dedotte da soli principi de ragione, dal P. lettore D. Antonmaria Gardini, monaco camaldalese, contro i materialisti e specialmente contro l'opera intitulata, le Bon-Sens, ou Idées Naturelles opposées aux idées Surnaturelles. In Padova MDCCLXXXI Nella stamperia del Seminario. Appresso Giovanni Manfré, Con Licenza de Superiori e Privilegio* (8vo, p. xx + 284).

---

[44] ["There is more than just common sense in this book, it is terrific. If it comes out of the same stable as *System of Nature*, the author has much improved". . . . "I agree with you on *Common Sense* which seems a much more formidable book than the *System of Nature*."]

14. In 1773 Holbach published his *Recherches sur les Miracles*, a much more sober work than his previous writings on religion. In this book he raises the well known difficulties with belief in miracles and brings a great deal of real learning and logic to bear on the question. The entire work is in a reasonable and philosophic spirit. His conclusion is that "une vraie religion doit avoir au défaut de bonnes raisons, des preuves sensibles, capables de faire impression sur tout ceux qui la cherchent de bonne foi. Ce ne sont pas les miracles."[45] The same year he published two serious but somewhat tiresome works on politics.

15. La politique naturelle.

16. *Système social* in which he attempts to reduce government to the naturalistic principles which were the basis of his entire philosophy. The first is also attributed to Malesherbes. There is a long and keen criticism of the *Système Social* by Mme. d'Epinay in a letter to Abbé Galiani Jan. 12, 1773 (Gal. *Corresp.*, Vol. II, p. 167).

But the most interesting reaction upon it was that of the Abbé Richard who criticized it from point of view of the divine right of kings in his long and tiresome work entitled *La Défense de la religion, de la morale, de la vertu, de la politique et de la société, dans la réfutation des ouvrages qui ont pour titre, l'un Système Social etc. l'autre La Politique Naturelle par le R. P. Ch. L. Richard, Professeur de Théologie*, etc., Paris, Moulard, 1775.

In a preface of forty-seven pages the fears of the conservative old Abbé are well expressed. The aim of these modern philosophers who are poisoning public opinion by their writings is to "démolir avec l'antique édifice de la religion chrétienne, celui des moeurs, de la vertu, de la saine politique etc. rompre tous les canaux de communication entre la terre et le

---

[45] ["a true religion must have, in the absence of reason, tangible pieces of evidence, capable of impressing everyone who is seeking in good faith. These are not miracles."]

ciel, bannir, exterminer du monde le Dieu qui le tira du néant, y introduire l'impiété la plus complète, la licence la plus consomnée, l'anarchie la plus entière, la confusion la plus horrible."[46]

17. Holbach's next work, *Ethocratie ou Gouvernement fondé sur la Morale*, Amsterdam, Rey, 1776, is interesting mainly for its unfortunate dedication and peroration, inscribed to Louis XVI, who was hailed therein as a long expected Messiah.

18. Holbach's last works dealt exclusively with morals. They are *La morale universelle ou les devoirs de l'homme fondés sur la nature*, Amsterdam, 1771, and

19. A posthumous work, *Elements de la Morale universelle, ou catechisme de la nature*, Paris, 1790. This is a beautiful little book. It is simple and clear to the last degree. There have been several translations in Spanish for the purposes of elementary education in morals in the public schools. It was composed in 1765. Holbach's attitude towards morals is indicated by his *Avertissement*—"La morale est une science dont les principes sont susceptibles d'une démonstration aussi claire et aussi rigoureuse que ceux du calcul et de la géometrie."[47]

---

[46] ["to demolish the antiquated edifice of the Christian religion, with its morals, virtue, political health etc., to break all channels of communication between earth and heaven, to banish, to destroy the world of the God who pulled it out of nothing, to introduce the most complete impiety, the most thorough license, the most complete anarchy, the most horrible confusion."]

[47] ["Morality is a science whose principles are susceptible to as clear and rigorous a demonstration as those of calculus and geometry."]

CHAPTER III.
THE SYSTÈME DE LA NATURE.

Early in 1770 appeared the famous Système de la Nature, ou Des Loix du Monde Physique et du Monde Morale, Par M. Mirabaud, Secrétaire Perpétuel et l'un des Quarante de l'Académie Française, Londres (Amsterdam), 1770. This work has gone through over thirty editions in France, Spain, Germany, England and the United States. No book of a philosophic or scientific character has ever caused such a sensation at the time of its publication, excepting perhaps Darwin's Origin of Species, the thesis of which is more than hinted at by Holbach. There were several editions in 1770. A very few copies contain a Discours préliminaire de l'Auteur of sixteen pages which Naigeon had printed separately in London. The Abrégé du Code de la Nature, which ends the book was also published separately and is sometimes attributed to Diderot, 8vo, 16 pp.[1]

There is also a book entitled *Le vrai sens du Système de la Nature*, 1774, attributed to Helvetius, a very clear, concise epitome largely in Holbach's own short and telling sentences, and much more effective than the original because of its brevity. Holbach himself reproduced the *Système de la Nature* in a shortened form in *Bon-sens*, 1772, and Payrard plagiarized it freely in *De la Nature et de ses Lois*, Paris, 1773. The book has been attributed to Diderot, Helvetius, Robinet, Damilaville and others. Naigeon is certain that it is entirely by Holbach, although it is generally held that Diderot had a hand in it. It was published

---

[1] Morley, *Diderot*, Vol. II, p. 155.

under the name of Mirabaud to obviate persecution. The manuscript, it was alleged, had been found among his papers as a sort of "testament" or philosophical legacy to posterity. This work may be called the bible of scientific materialism and dogmatic atheism. Nothing before or since has ever approached it in its open and unequivocal insistence on points of view commonly held, if at all, with reluctance and reserve. It is impossible in a study of this length to deal fully with the attacks and refutations that were published immediately. We may mention first the condemnation of the book by the *Parlement de Paris*, August 18, 1770, to be burned by the public hangman along with Voltaire's *Dieu et les Hommes*, and Holbach's *Discours sur les Miracles*, *La Contagion sacrée* and *le Christianisme dévoilé*, which had already been condemned on September 24, 1769.[2]

The *Réquisitoire* of Seguier, *avocat général*, on the occasion of the condemnation of the *Système de la Nature* was so weak and ridiculous that the *Parlement de Paris* refused to sanction its publication, and it was printed by the express order of the King. As Grimm observed, it seemed designed solely to acquaint the ignorant with this dangerous work, without opposing any of its propositions. One would look in vain for a better example of the conservatism of the legal profession.[3]

Le poison des nouveautés profanes ne peut corrompre la sainte gravité des moeurs qui caractérise les vrais Magistrats: tout peut changer autour d'eux, *ils restent immuables avec la loi* (page 496).

N'est-ce pas ce fatal abus de la liberté de penser, qui a enfanté cette multitude de sectes, d'opinions, de partis, et cet esprit d'indépendance dont d'autres nations ont éprouvé les sinstres révolutions. Le même abus produira en France des effets

---

[2] Later *Bon-sens* and *Théologie portative* were doomed to the flames by the condemnations of Jan. 10, 1774, and February 16, 1776.

[3] *Système de la Nature*, ed. 1771, Vol. II, p. 496.

peut-être plus funestes. La liberté indéfinie trouveroit, dans la caractère de la nation, dans son activité, dans son amour pour la nouveauté, un moyen de plus pour préparer les plus affreuses révolutions[4] (p. 498).

The most interesting private attacks on the *Système de la Nature* came from two somewhat unexpected quarters, from Ferney and Sans Souci. Voltaire, as usual, was not wholly consistent in his opinions of it, as is revealed in his countless letters on the subject. Grimm attributed his hostility to jealousy, and the fear that the *Système de la Nature* might "renverse le rituel de Ferney et que le patriarcat ne s'en aille au diable avec lui."[5] George Leroy went so far as to write a book entitled *Réflexions sur la jalousie, pour servir de commentaire aux derniers ouvrages de M. de Voltaire*, 1772. Frederick II naturally felt bound to defend the kings who, as Voltaire said, were no better treated than God in the *Système de la Nature*.[6]

Voltaire's correspondence during this period is so interesting that it seems worth while to quote at length, especially from his letters to Fredrick the Great. In May 1770, shortly after the publication of the *Système de la Nature* Voltaire wrote to M. Vernes:[7] "On a tant dit de sottises sur la nature que je ne lis plus

---

[4] [The poison of profane novelties cannot corrupt the sacred seriousness of the morals which characterize true Magistrates: everything can change around them, they stay unchanged within the law ...

. . . Isn't it this fatal abuse of freedom of thought, which gave birth to the multitude of sects, opinions, parties, and that spirit of independence that caused other nations to experience dire revolutions? The same abuse in France may produce even more disastrous effects. Unlimited freedom would promote in the character of the nation, in its activity, in his love of novelty, one more way to bring about the most terrible revolutions.]

[5] Grimm, *Cor. Lit.*, Vol. IX, p. 167.

["knock down Ferney's ritual so that the patriarchy would not go to the devil with him"]

[6] Voltaire, *Oeuvres*, ed. Beuchot, Vol. LXVI, p. 404. Subsequent references to Voltaire are from this edition.

[7] Vol. LXVII, p. 265.

aucun de ces livres là."[8] But by July he had read it and wrote to Grimm:[9] "Si l'ouvrage eut été plus serré il aurait fait un effet terrible, mais tel qu'il est il en a fait beaucoup. Il est bien plus éloquent que Spinoza... J'ai une grande curiosité de savoir ce qu'on en pense à Paris."[10] In writing to d'Alembert about this time he seemed to have a fairly favorable impression of the book. "Il m'a paru qu'il y avait des longueurs, des répétitions et quelques inconséquences, mais il y a trop de bon pour qu'on n'éclate avec fureur contre ce livre. Si on garde le silence, ce sera une preuve du prodigieux progrès que la tolérance fait tous les jours."[11] But there was little likelihood that philosophers or theologians would keep silent about this scandalous book. Before the end of the month Voltaire was writing to d'Alembert about his own and the king of Prussia's refutations of it, and the same day wrote to Frederick: "Il me semble que vos remarques doivent être imprimées; ce sont des leçons pour le genre humain. Vous soutenez d'un bras la cause de Dieu et vous écrasez de l'autre la superstition."[12] Later Voltaire confessed to Frederick that he also had undertaken to rebuke the author of the Système de la Nature. "Ainsi Dieu a pour lui les deux hommes les moins

---

[8] ["So much nonsense has been said about the *Nature* that I am not reading any of it"]

[9] Grimm, *Cor. Lit.*, Vol. IX, p. 90.

[10] ["If the book had been tighter it would have had a tremendous effect, but as it is, he has done a lot. It is much more eloquent than Spinoza ... I am very curious to know what people in Paris think of it."]

[11] Vol. LXVI, p. 432.

["It seemed to me that there were longueurs, repetitions and some inconsistencies, but there is too much good for people not to erupt with fury against this book. If they stay silent, it will be a proof of the extraordinary progress that tolerance makes every day."]

[12] Vol. LXVI, p. 563.

["I think your comments should be printed, these are lessons for mankind. You raise one arm to support God and the other to crush superstition."]

superstitieux de l'Europe, ce que devrait lui plaire beaucoup"[13] (p. 390).

Frederick, however, hesitated to make his refutation public, and wrote to Voltaire: "Lorsque j'eus achevé mon ouvrage contre l'athéisme, je crus ma réfutation très orthodoxe, je la relus, et je la trouvai bien éloignée de l'être. Il y a des endroits qui ne saurait paraître sans effaroucher les timides et scandaliser les dévots. Un petit mot qui m'est échappé sur l'éternité du monde me ferait lapider dans votre patrie, si j'y étais né particulier, et que je l'eusse fait imprimer. Je sens que je n'ai point du tout ni l'âme ni le style théologique."[14] Voltaire, in his "petite drôlerie en faveur de la Divinité" (as he called his work) and in his letters, could not find terms harsh enough in which to condemn the *Système de la Nature*. He called it "un chaos, un grand mal moral, un ouvrage de ténèbres, un péché contre la nature, un système de la folie et de l'ignorance," and wrote to Delisle de Sales: "Je ne vois pas que rien ait plus avili notre siècle que cette énorme sottise."[15] Voltaire seemed to grow more bitter about Holbach's book as time went on. His letters and various works abound in references to it, and it is difficult to determine his motives. He was accused, as has been suggested, by Holbach's circle "de caresser les gens en place, et

---

[13] ["So God has on his side the two least superstitious men in Europe, that should please him greatly"]

[14] Vol. LXVI, p. 386.

["When I finished my book against atheism, I thought my refutation very orthodox; I reread it, and I found it a long way from being so. There are some matters that cannot appear without startling the timid and scandalizing the devout. A little word that escaped me on the eternity of the world could get me stoned in your country, if I had been born peculiar, and had had it printed. I feel that I have nothing at all, neither the soul nor the theological style."]

[15] Vol. LXVI, p. 394.

["a chaos, a great moral evil, a work of darkness, a sin against nature, a system of folly and ignorance, . . . I do not see anything that has debased our century more than this enormous stupidity."]

d'abandonner ceux qui n'y sont plus."[16] M. Avenel believed that he suspected Holbach himself of making these accusations. Voltaire's letter to the Duc de Richelieu, Nov. 1, 1770,[17] seems to give them foundation.

A very different reaction was that of Goethe and his university circle at Strasburg to whom the *Système de la Nature* appeared a harmless and uninteresting book, "grau," "cimmerisch," "totenhaft," "die echte Quintessenz der Greisenheit." To these fervent young men in the youthful flush of romanticism, its sad, atheistic twilight seemed to cast a veil over the beauty of the earth and rob the heaven of stars; and they lightheardedly discredited both Holbach and Voltaire in favor of Shakespeare and the English romantic school. One would look far for a better instance of the romantic reaction which set in so soon and so obscured the clarity of the issues at stake in the eighteenth century thought.[18]

---

[16] Vol. XXVIII, p. 493.

["soothing the people on the spot, and abandoning those who have left"]

[17] Vol. LXVI, p. 469.

[18] Goethe, *Wahrheit und Dichtung*, 11th Book, Goethe's *Werke*, Stuttgart, Vol. 19, p. 55.

Auf philosophische Weise erleuchtet und gefödert zu werden, hatten wir keinen Trieb noch Hang: über religiöse Gegenstände glaubten wir uns selbst aufgeklärt zu haben, und so war der heftige Streit französischer Philosophen mit dem Pfafftum uns ziemlich gleichgültig. Verbotene, zurn Feuer verdaminte Bücher, welche damals grossen Lärmen machten, übten keine Wirkung auf uns. Ich gedenke statt aller des *Système de la Nature*, das wir aus Neugier in die Hand nahmen. Wir begriffen nicht, wie ein solches Buch gefährlich sein könnte. Es kam uns so grau, so cimmerisch, so totenhaft vor, das wir Mühe hatten, seine Gegenwart auszuhalten, dass wir davor wie vor einern Gespenste schauderten. Der Verfasser glaubt sein Buch ganz eigens zu empfehlen, wenn er in der Vorrede versichert, dass er, als ein abgelebter Greis, soeben in die Grube stiegend, der Mit- und Nachwelt die Wahrheit verkünden wolle. Wir lachten ihn aus: denn wir glaubten bemerkt zu haben, dass von alten Leuten eigentlich an der Welt nichts geschätzt werde, was liebenswürdig und gut an ihr ist. "Alte Kirchen haben dunkle Gläser" "Wie Kirschen und Beeren schmecken, muss mann Kinder und Sperlinge fragen"—

dies waren unsere Lust und Leibworte: und so schien uns jenes Buch, als die rechte Quintessenz der Greisenheit, unschmachhaft, ja abgeschmackt Alles sollte notwendig sein und deswegen kein Gott. "Könnte es denn aber nicht auch notwendig einen Gott geben?" fragten wir. Dabei gestanden wir freilich, das wir uns den Notwendigkeiten der Tage und Nächte, der Jahrszeiten, der klirnatischen Einflusse, der physichen und animalischen Zustände nicht wohl entziehen könnten: doch fühlten wir etwas in uns, das als vollkommene Willkür erschien, und wieder etwas, das sich mit dieser Willkür ins Gleichgewicht zu setzen suchte. Die Hoffnung, immer vernünftiger zu werden, uns von den aussern Dingen, ja von uns selbst immer unabhängiger zu machen, konnten wir nicht aufgeben. Das Wort Freiheit klingt so schon, dass mann es nicht entbehren könnte und wenn es einen Irrtum bezeichnete.

Keiner von uns hatte das Buch hinausgelesen; denn wir fanden uns in der Erwartung getäuscht, in der wir es auf geschlagen hatten. *System der Natur* ward angekündigt und wir hofften also wirklich etwas von der Natur, unsere Abgötten, zu erfahren. Physik und Chemie, Himmels- und Erdbeschriebung, Naturgeschichte und Anatomie und so manches andere hatte nun zeit Jahren und bis auf den letzten Tag uns immer auf die geschmüchte grosse Welt hingeweisen, und wir hatten gern von Sonnen und Sternen, von Planeten und Monden, von Bergen, Thälern, Flüssen und Meeren und von allem, was dann lebt und webt, das Nähere sowie das Allgemeinere erfahren. Das hierbei wohl manches vorkommen müsste, was dem gemeinen Menschen als schädlich, der Geistlichkeit als gefährlich, dem Staat als unzulässig erschienen möchte, daran hatten wir keinen Zweifel, und wir hofften, dieses Büchlein sollte nicht unwürdig die Feuerprobe bestauden haben. Allein wie hohl und leer ward uns in deiser tristen Atheistischen Halbnacht zu Mute, in welcher die Erde mit allen ihren Gebilden, der Himmel mit allen seinen Gestirnen verschwand! Eine Materie sollte sein von Ewigkeit und von Ewigkeit her bewegt, und sollte nun mit dieser Bewegung rechts und links und nach allen Seiten ohne weiteres die unendlichen Phänomene des Daseins hervorbringen. Dies alles wären wir sogar zufrieden gewesen, wenn der Verfasser wirklich aus seiner bewegten Materie die Welt vor unsern Augen aufgebaut hätte. Aber er mochte von der Natur so wenig wissen als wir; denn indem er einige allgemeine Begriffe hingepfahlt, verlässt er sie sogleich, um dasjenige, was höher als die Natur oder als höhere Natur in der Natur erschient, zur materiellen schweren, zwar bewegten, aber doch richtungs- und gestaltlosen Natur zu verwandeln, und glaubt dadurch recht viel gewonnen zu haben. Wenn uns jedoch dieses Buch einigen Schaden gebracht hat, so war es der, das wir allen Philosophie, besonderers aber der Metaphysick recht herzlich gram wurden, und bleiben, dagegen aber auf lebendige Wissen, Erfahren, Thun und Dichten uns nur desto lebhafter und leidenschaftlicher hinwarfen.

[Translation: We had neither impulse nor tendency to be illumined and advanced in a philosophical manner: on religious subjects we thought we had sufficiently enlightened ourselves, and therefore the violent contest of the French philosophers with the priesthood was tolerably indifferent to us. Prohibited books, condemned to the flames, which then made a great noise, produced no effect upon us. I mention as an instance, to serve for all, the "Système de la Nature," which we took in hand out of curiosity. We did not understand how such a book could be dangerous. It appeared to us so dark, so Cimmerian, so deathlike, that we found it a trouble to endure its presence, and shuddered at it as at a spectre. The author fancies he gives his book a peculiar recommendation, when he declares in his preface, that as a decrepit old man, just sinking into he grave, he wishes to announce the truth to his contemporaries and to posterity.

We laughed at him; for we thought we had observed, that by old people nothing in the world that is lovable and good is, in fact, appreciated. "Old churches have dark windows: to know how cherries and berries taste, we must ask children and sparrows." These were our gibes and maxims; and thus that book, as the very quintessence of senility, appeared to us as unsavoury, nay, absurd. "All was to be of necessity," so said the book, "and therefore there was no God." But might not there be a God by necessity too? asked we. We indeed confessed, at the same time, that we could not withdraw ourselves from the necessities of day and night, the seasons, the influence of climate, physical and animal condition : we nevertheless felt within us something that appeared like perfect freedom of will, and again something which endeavoured to counterbalance this freedom. The hope of becoming more and more rational, of making ourselves more and more independent of external things, nay, of ourselves, we could not give up. The word freedom sounds so beautiful, that we cannot do without it, even though it should designate an error.

Not one of us had read the book through, for we found ourselves deceived in the expectations with which we had opened it. A system of nature was announced; and therefore we hoped to learn really something of nature, — our idol. Physics and chemistry, descriptions of heaven and earth, natural history and anatomy, with much else, had now for years, and up to the last day, constantly directed us to the great, adorned world; and we would willingly have heard both particulars and generals about suns and stars, planets and moons, mountains, valleys, rivers and seas, with all that live and move in them. That, in the course of this, much must occur which would appear to the common man as injurious, to the clergy as dangerous, and to the state as inadmissible, we had no doubt; and we hoped that the little book had not unworthily stood the fiery ordeal. But how hollow and empty did we feel

The leading refutations directed explicitly against the *Système de la Nature* are:

1. 1770, Rive, Abbé J. J., Lettres philosophiques contre le *Système de la Nature*. (Portefeuille hebdomadaire de Bruxelles.)
2. Frederick II, *Examen critique du livre intitulé, Système de la Nature*. (Political Miscellanies, p. 175.)
3. Voltaire, Dieu, Réponse de M. de Voltaire au *Système de la Nature*. Au château de Ferney, 1770, 8 vo, pp. 34.
4. 1771, Bergier, Abbé N. F., Examen du matérialisme, ou Réfutation du *Système de la Nature*. Paris, Humbolt, 1771, 2 vols., 12mo.
5. Camuset, Abbé J. N., Principes contre l'incrédulité, a l'occasion du *Système de la Nature*. Paris, Pillot, 1771, 12mo, pp. viii + 335.
6. Castillon, J. de (Salvernini di Castiglione), Observations sur le livre intitulé, *Système de la Nature*. Berlin, Decker, 1771, 8vo. (40 sols broché.)
7. Rochford, Dubois de, Pensées diverses contre le système des matérialistes, à l'occasion d'un écrit intitulé; *Système de la Nature*. Paris, Lambert, 1771, 12mo.

---

in this melancholy, atheistical halfnight, in which earth vanished with all its images, heaven with all its stars. There was to be a matter in motion from all eternity; and by this motion, right and left and in every direction, without anything further, it was to produce the infinite phenomena of existence. Even all this we should have allowed to pass, if the author, out of his moved matter, had really built up the world before our eyes. But he seemed to know as little about nature as we did; for, having set up some general ideas, he quits them at once, for the sake of changing that which appears as higher than nature, or as a higher nature within nature, into material, heavy nature, which is moved, indeed, but without direction or form — and thus he fancies he has gained a great deal. If, after all, this book had done us some harm, it was this, — that we took a hearty dislike to all philosophy, and especially metaphysics, and remained in that dislike; while, on the other hand, we threw ourselves into living knowledge, experience, action, and poetising, with all the more liveliness and passion.]

8. 1773, L'Impie démasqué, ou remontrance aux écrivains incrédules. Londres, Heydinger, 1773
9. Holland, J. H., Réflexions philosophiques sur le *Système de la Nature*. Paris, 1773, 2 vols., 8vo.
10. 1776, Buzonnière, Nouel de, Observations sur un ouvrage intitulé le *Système de la Nature*. Paris, Debure, père, 1776, 8vo, pp. 126. (Prix 1 livre, 16 sols broché.)
11. 1780, Fangouse, Abbé, La religion prouvée aux incrédules, avec une lettre à l'auteur du *Système de la Nature* par un homme du monde. Paris, Debure l'aîné, 12mo, p. 150. Same under title Réflexions importantes sur la religion, etc., 1785.
12. 1788, Paulian, A. J., Le véritable système de la nature, etc., Avignon, Niel, 2 vols., 12mo.
13. 1803, Mangold, F. X. von, Unumstossliche Widerlegung des Materialismus gegen den Verfasser des *Systems der Natur*. Augsburg, 1803.

Of these and other refutations of materialism such as Saint-Martin's *Des erreurs et de la vérité*, Dupont de Nemours' *Philosophie de l'univers*, Delisles de Sales' *Philosophie de la nature*, etc., which are not directed explicitly against the *Système de la Nature*, the works of Voltaire and Frederick the Great are the most interesting but by no means the most serious or convincing. Morley finds Voltaire very weak and much beside the point, especially in his discussion of order and disorder in nature which Holbach had denied. Voltaire's argument is that there must be an intelligent motor or cause behind nature (p. 7). This is God (p. 8). He admits at the outset that all systems are mere dreams but he continues to insist with a dogmatism equal to Holbach's on the validity of his dream. He repeatedly asserts without foundation that Holbach's system is based on the false experiment of Needham (pp. 5, 6), and even goes so far as to ridicule the evolutionary hypothesis altogether (p. 6). He speaks of the necessity of a belief in God, by a kind of natural logic. God and matter exist in the nature of things, "Tout nous announce un Être suprême, rien ne nous dit ce qu'il est." God himself seems to be a kind of fatalistic necessity. "C'est ce que vous appellerez Nature et c'est ce que j'appelle Dieu."[19] At the end he shifts the argument from the base of necessity to that of utility. Which is the more consoling doctrine? If the idea of God has prevented ten crimes I hold that the entire world should embrace it (p. 27). As Morley has said, such arguments could scarcely have convinced Voltaire himself.

Frederick was surprised that Voltaire and D'Alembert had found anything good in the book. His refutation was more methodical than that of Voltaire, who called it a "homage to the Divinity" but wrote to D'Alembert that it was written in the style of a notary. Two other refutations emanating from the Academy of Berlin were those of Castillon and Holland. The first of these is a very heavy and learned work, formidable and forbidding in its logic. Castillon reduces Holbach's propositions to three. The self-existence of matter, the essential relation of movement to it, and the possibility of deriving everything from it or some mode of it. Castillon concludes after five hundred pages of reasoning that matter is contingent, movement not inherent in it, and that purely spiritual beings exist in independence of it. Hence the *Système de la Nature* is a "long and wicked error." Holland's is a still more serious work, which the Sorbonne recommended strongly as an antidote against Holbach's *Système* which it qualified as "une malheureuse production que notre siècle doit rougir d'avoir enfantée."[20] But when it was discovered that Holland was a Protestant his work was condemned forthwith, Jan. 17, 1773.

Bergier's refutation is interesting as an attack from a churchman of extraordinary keenness and insight into the progress of the new philosophy. In the *Système de la Nature* he

[19] ["Everything speaks of a Supreme Being, nothing tells us what it is. . . . That which you call Nature, I call God."]

[20] ["a wretched production that our century should blush to have begotten."]

recognized the hand of the author of *La Contagion sacrée* and the *Essai sur les préjugés* and dealt with it as he did the *Christianisme dévoilé*. Buzonniere, Rochfort and Fangouse are milder and more naive in their demonstrations and their works are of no weight or interest. *L'Impie démasqué* is a brutal work which qualifies Holbach as a "vile apostle of vice and crime," and the *Système de la Nature* as the most impudent treatise on atheism that has yet dishonored the globe—one which covers the century with shame and will be the scandal of future generations.

The work of Paulian is of a different sort. Coming comparatively late, it attempted to review the hostile opinions of many years and then mass them in an overwhelming final attack on the *Système de la Nature*. To this end Paulian rewrites the entire book chapter by chapter, giving the "true version." He then reviews Holland's outline and Bergier's comments, together with seven articles directed explicitly against the *Système de la Nature* in such works as the *Lettres Helviennes*, of Abbé Barruel, *Dict. des Philosophes*, *Dict. anti-philosophe*, his own *Dict. théologique*, etc., besides many other writings against the new philosophy in general. He then reviews articles by members of the philosophic school against materialism and then goes back to Holbach's sources, Diderot, Bayle, Spinoza, Lucretius, Epicurus, etc. The work is not scholarly but comprehensive and evidently discouraged further formal refutations.

The *Système de la Nature* had many critics in the stormy days that followed 1789. Delisle de Sales found it a monstrosity—a *fratras*; La Harpe called it an infamous book, "un amas de bêtises qu'on ose appeler philosophie, inconcevables inepties, un immense échafaudage de mensonge et d'invective"[21]; M. Villemain is much more calm and fair; Lord Brougham, like Damiron, Buzonnière, and many others,

---

[21] ["a heap of nonsense they dare call philosophy, inconceivable absurdities, a huge scaffolding of lies and invective"]

found it seductive but full of false reasoning; Lerminier was so severe that St.-Beuve was moved to defend Holbach against him. Samuel Wilkinson, the English translator of 1820, is one of the few whose criticism is at all favorable. Holbach has always appealed to a certain type of radical mind and his translators and editors have generally been men who were often over-enthusiastic. For example, Mr. Wilkinson says of the *Système de la Nature*,[22] "No work, ancient or modern, has surpassed it in the eloquence and sublimity of its language or in the facility with which it treats the most abstruse and difficult subjects. It is without exception the boldest effort the human mind has yet produced in the investigation of Morals and Theology. The republic of letters has never produced another author whose pen was so well calculated to emancipate mankind from all those trammels with which the nurse, the school master, and the priest have successively locked up their noblest faculties, before they were capable of reasoning and judging for themselves."

It seems unnecessary to analyze the *Système de la Nature*. This has been done by Damiron, Soury, Fabre, Lange, Morley, the historians of philosophy, and encyclopaedists; and the book itself is easily available in the larger libraries. The substance of Holbach's philosophy is susceptible of clearer treatment apart from it or any one of his books, although it permeates all of them.

M. Jules Soury has said, in describing a certain type of mind: "Il est d'heureux esprits, des âmes fortes et saines, que n'effraie point le silence éternel des espaces infinis où s'anéantissait la raison de Pascal. Naïves et robustes natures, mâles et vigoureux penseurs, qui gardent toute la vie quelque chose des dons charmants de la jeunesse et de l'enfance même, une foi vive dans le témoinage immédiat de nos sens et de notre conscience, une humeur alerte, toute de joyeuse ardeur, et comme une intrépidité d'esprit que rien n'arrête. Pour eux tout est clair et

[22] Vol. II, p. 261, ed. 1820.

uni; ou à peu près, et là où ils soupçonnent quelque bas-bond insondable, ils se détournent et poursuivent fièrement leur chemin. Comme cet Epicurien dont parle Cicéron au commencement du *De natura deorum*, ils ont toujours l'air de sortir de l'assemblée des dieux et de descendre des intermondes d'Epicure."[23]

Such was Holbach. His philosophy is based on the child-like assumption that things are as they seem, provided they are observed with sufficient care by a sufficient number of people. This brings us at once to the very heart of Holbach's method which was experimental and inductive to the last degree. Holbach was nourished on what might be called scientific rather than philosophical traditions. As M. Tourneux has pointed out, he had been a serious student of the natural sciences, especially those connected with the constitution of the earth. These studies led him to see the disparity between certain accepted and traditional cosmologies and a scientific interpretation of the terrestrial globe and the forms of life which flourish upon it. Finding the supposed sacred and infallible records untrustworthy in one regard, he began to question their veracity at other points. Being of a critical frame of mind, he took the records rather more literally than a sympathetic, allegorical apologist would have done, although it cannot be said that he used much historical insight. After having studied the sacred texts for purposes of writing or having translated other men's studies on

---

[23] ["Happy spirited, strong in soul and healthy is the man undismayed by the eternal silence of infinite spaces which annihilated Pascal's reason. Naive and robust natures, masculine and vigorous thinkers, who preserve something of the charming gifts of adolescence and even childhood throughout their lives, have a living faith in the immediate witness of their senses and consciousness, an alert outlook, full of joyful ardor, and an intrepid mind that nothing can stop. For them everything is clear and plain, or nearly so, and where they suspect some unfathomable leap, they turn away and continue on their way proudly. As the Epicurean mentioned at the beginning of Cicero's *De natura deorum*, they always seem to have just left the assembly of the gods and descended to the in-between worlds of Epicurus."]

Moses, David, the Prophets, Jesus, Paul, the Christian theologians and saints, miracles, etc., he concluded that these accounts were untrustworthy and mendacious. He knew ancient and modern philosophy and found in the greater part of it an unwarranted romantic or theological trend which his scientific training had caused him to suspect. It must be admitted that however false or illogical Holbach's conclusions may be considered, he was by no means ignorant of the subjects he chose to treat, as some of his detractors would have one believe. His theory of knowledge was that of Locke and Condillac, and on this foundation he built up his system of scientific naturalism and dogmatic atheism.

His initial assumption is, as has been suggested, that experience (application réitérée des sens) and reason are trustworthy guides to knowledge. By them we become conscious of an external objective world, of which sentient beings themselves are a part, from which they receive impressions through their sense organs. These myriad impressions when compared and reflected upon form reasoned knowledge or truth, provided they are substantiated by repeated experiences carefully made. That is, an idea is said to be true when it conforms perfectly with the actual external object. This is possible unless one's senses are defective, or one's judgment vitiated by emotion and passion.

Holbach's contention is that if one applies experience and reason to the external universe, or nature, "ce vaste assemblage de tout ce qui existe"[24]; it reveals a *single objective reality*, i. e., *matter*, which is in itself essentially active or in a state of motion.

From matter in motion are derived all the phenomena that strike our senses. All is matter or a function of it. Matter, then, is not an effect, but a cause. It is not caused; it is from eternity and of necessity. The cardinal point in Holbach's philosophy is an

---

[24] ["that vast assemblage of all that exists"]

inexorable materialistic necessity. Nothing, then, is exempt from the laws of physics and chemistry. Inorganic substance and organic life fall into the same category. Man himself with all his differentiated faculties is but a function of matter and motion in extraordinary complex and involved relations. Man's imputation to himself of free will and unending consciousness apart from his machine is an idle tale built on his desires, not on his experiences nor his knowledge of nature. This imputation of a will or soul to nature, independent of it or in any sense above it, is a still more idle one derived from his renunciation of the witness of his senses and his following after the phantoms of his imagination. It is ignorance or disregard of nature then that has given rise to supernatural ideas that have "no correspondence with true sight," or, as Holbach expressed it, have no counterpart in the external object. In other words, theology, or poetry about God, as Petrarch said, is ignorance of natural causes reduced to a system.

Man is a purely natural or physical being, like a tree or a stone. His so-called spiritual nature (l'homme moral) is merely a phase of his physical nature considered under a special aspect. He is all matter in motion, and when that ceases to function in a particular way, called life, he ceases to be as a conscious entity. He is so organized, however that his chief desires are to survive and render his existence happy. By happiness Holbach means the presence of pleasure and the absence of pain. In all his activity, then, man will seek pleasure and avoid pain. The chief cause of man's misery or lack of well being is his ignorance of the powers and possibilities of his own nature and the Universal Nature. All he needs is to ascertain his place in nature and adjust himself to it. From the beginning of his career he has been the dupe of false ideas, especially those connected with supernatural powers, on whom he supposed he was dependent. But, if ignorance of nature gave birth to the Gods, knowledge of nature is calculated to destroy them and the evils resulting from them, the introduction of theistic ideas into politics and morals. In a word, the truth, that is, *correct ideas of nature* is the one thing needful to the happiness and well-being of man.

The application of these principles to the given situation in France in 1770 would obviously have produced unwelcome results. Holbach's theory was that religion was worse than useless in that it had inculcated false and pernicious ideas in politics and morals. He would do away completely with it in the interest of putting these sciences on a natural basis. This basis is self-interest, or man's inevitable inclination toward survival and the highest degree of well-being, "L'objet de la morale est de faire connaître aux hommes que leur plus grand intérêt exige qu'ils pratiquent la vertu; le but du gouvernement doit être de la leur faire pratiquer."[25]

Government then assumes the functions of moral restraint formally delegated to religion; and punishments render virtue attractive and vice repugnant. Holbach's theory of social organization is practically that of Aristotle. Men combine in order to increase the store of individual well-being, to live the good life. If those to whom society has delegated sovereignty abuse their power, society has the right to take it from them. Sovereignty is merely an agent for the diffusion of truth and the maintenance of virtue, which are the prerequisites of social and individual well-being. The technique of progress is enlightenment and good laws.

Nothing could be clearer or simpler than Holbach's system. As Diderot so truly said, he will not be quoted on both sides of any question. His uncompromising atheism is the very heart and core of his system and clarifies the whole situation. All supernatural ideas are to be abandoned. Experience and reason are once for all made supreme, and henceforth refuse to share their throne or abdicate in favor of faith. Holbach's aim was as

---

[25] ["The purpose of morality is to make men know that it is in their best interest to practice virtue, the government's goal should be to make them practice it."]

he said to bring man back to nature and render reason dear to him. "Il est tempts que cette raison injustement dégradée quitte un ton pusillamine qui la rendront complice du mensonge et du délire."[26]

If reason is to rule, the usurper, religion, must be ejected; hence atheism was fundamental to his entire system. He did not suppose by any means that it would become a popular faith, because it presupposed too much learning and reflection, but it seemed to him the necessary weapon of a reforming party at that time. He defines an atheist as follows: "C'est un homme, qui détruit des chimères nuisibles au genre humain, pour ramener les hommes à la nature, à l'expérience, à la raison. C'est un penseur qui, ayant médité la matière, ses propriétés et ses façons d'agir, n'a pas besoin, pour expliquer les phénomènes de l'univers et les opérations de la nature, d'imaginer des puissances idéales, des intelligences imaginaires, des êtres de raison; qui loin de faire mieux connaître cette nature, ne font que la rendre capricieuse, inexplicable, et méconnaissable, inutile au bonheur des hommes."[27]

---

[26] ["It is time that such unjustly degraded reason abandons its pusillanimous tone which rendered it complicit in lies and delusions."]

[27] ["He is a man who destroys chimeras harmful to mankind, to bring men back to nature, experience, reason. He is a thinker who, having pondered the material world, its properties and ways of behaving, does not need to explain the phenomena of the universe and the operations of nature by imagining ideal powers, imaginary intelligences, beings of reason; which rather than making one understand that nature better, merely render it capricious, inexplicable, and unrecognizable, unfit for human happiness."]

Appendix. Holbach's Correspondence

The following letters of Holbach are extant:

Holbach to Hume, Aug. 23, 1763.

Holbach to Hume, Mar. 16, 1766.

Holbach to Hume, July 7, 1766.

Holbach to Hume, Aug. 18, 1766.

Holbach to Hume, Sept. 7, 1766.

These were printed in Hume's Private Correspondence, London, 1820, pp. 252-263, and deal largely with Hume's quarrel with Rousseau.

Holbach to Garrick, June 16, 1765.

Holbach to Garrick, Feb. 9, 1766.

These two letters are in manuscript in Lansdowne House, Coll. Forster, and were published by F. A. Hedgcock, *David Garrick et ses amis français*. Paris, 1911, pp. 251-253.

Holbach to Wilkes, Aug., 1746, 9 (Brit. Mus. Mss., Vol. 30867, p. 14).

Holbach to Wilkes, Dec. 10, 1746 (Brit. Mus. Mss., Vol. 30867, p. 18).

Holbach to Wilkes, May 22, 1766 (Brit. Mus. Mss., Vol. 30869, p. 39)

Holbach to Wilkes, Nov. 9, 1766 (Brit. Mus. Mss., Vol. 30869, p. 81).

Holbach to Wilkes, Dec. 10, 1767 (Brit. Mus. Mss., Vol. 30869, p. 173).

Holbach to Wilkes, July 17, 1768 (Brit. Mus. Mss., Vol. 30870, p. 59).

Holbach to Wilkes, Mar. 19, 1770 (Brit. Mus. Mss., Vol. 30871, p. 16).

Holbach to Wilkes, April 27, 1775, 9 (Wilkes, *Correspondence*, London, 1804, Vol. IV, p. 176).

The first seven of these letters are published for the first time in the present volume, pp. 6-11 and pp. 75-80.

Holbach to Galiani, Aug. 11, 1769 (*Critica*, Vol. I, pp. 488 sq.).

Galiani to Holbach, April 7, 1770 (Galiani, *Correspondence*, Paris, 1890, Vol. I, p. 92).

Galiani to Holbach, July 21, 1770 (Galiani, *Correspondence*, Paris, 1890, Vol. I, p. 199).

Holbach to Galiani, Aug. 25, 1770 (*Critica*, Vol. I, p. 489).

There are references to other letters in *Critica* which I have not been able to find.

Holbach to Beccaria, Mar. 15, 1767, published by M. Landry Beccaria, Scritte e lettre inediti, 1910, p. 146.

Holbach to Malesherbes, April 6, 1761 (hitherto unpublished). See present volume, p. 32.

HOLBACH TO HUME

(Hume, Private Correspondence, London, 1820, pp. 252-263)

PARIS, the 23rd. of August, 1763

Sir,—

I have received with the deepest sense of gratitude your very kind and obliging letter of the 8th. inst: favors of great men ought to give pride to those that have at least the merit of setting the value that is due upon them. This is my case with you, sir; the reading of your valuable works has not only inspired me with the strongest admiration for your genius and amiable parts, but gave me the highest idea of your person and the strongest desire of getting acquainted with one of the greatest philosophers of my age, and of the best friend to mankind. These sentiments have emboldened me to send formally, though unknown to you, the work you are mentioning to me. I thought you were the best to judge of such a performance, and I took only the liberty of giving a hint of my desires, in case it should meet with your approbation, nor was I surprized, or presumed to be displeased, at seeing my wishes disappointed. The reasons appeared very obvious to me; not withstanding the British liberty, I conceived there were limits even to it. However, my late friend's book has appeared since and there is even an edition of it lately done in England: I believe it will be relished by the friends of truth, who like to see vulgar errors struck at the root. This has been your continued task, sir; and you deserve for it the praises of all sincere wellwishers of humanity: give me leave to rank myself among them, and express to you, by this opportunity you have been so kind as to give me, the fervent desire we have to see you in this country. Messrs. Stuart, Dempster, Fordyce, who are so good as to favor me with their company, have given me some hopes of seeing you in this metropolis, where you have so many admirers as readers, and as many sincere friends as there are disciples of philosophy. I don't doubt but my good friend M. Helvétius will join in our wishes, and prevail upon you to come over. I assure you, sir, you won't perceive much the change of the country, for all countries are alike for people that have the same minds.

I am, with the greatest veneration and esteem, sir, your most obedient and most humble servant.

D'HOLBACH.

Rue Royale, butte St. Roch, à Paris.

HOLBACH TO GARRICK

(Coll. Forster, Vol. XXI; pub., Hedgcock, p. 253)

PARIS, Feb ye 9 th, 1766.

I received, my very Dear Sir, with a great deal of pleasure, your agreeable letter of ye 24th of January, but was very sorry to hear that you are inlisted in the numerous troup of gouty people. Tho' I have myself the honour of being of that tribe I dont desire my friends should enter into the same corporation. I am particularly griev'd to see you among the invalids for you have, more than any other, occasion for the free use of your limbs. However, don't be cross and peevish for that would be only increasing you distemper; and I charge you especially of not scolding that admirable lady Mrs Garrick, whose sweetness of temper and care must be a great comfort in your circumstances. I beg leave to present her with my respects and ye compliments of my wife, that has enjoyed but an indifferent state of health, owing to the severity of the winter. M^{r} and Mad^{e} Helvetius desire you both their best wishes and so do all your friends, for whom I can answer that every one of them keeps a kind remembrance of your valuable persons. Dr. Gem thinks you'll do very well to go to Bath, but his opinion is that a thin diet would be more serviceable to you than anything else; believe he is in the right. Abbé Morellet pays many thanks for the answers to his queries, but complains of their shortness and laconism; however it is not your fault. He is glad to hear you have receiv'd his translation of Beccaria's book, *Des délits et des peines* and the compliments of our friend Dr Gatti to whom I gave your direction before he went to London. Our friend Suard has entered his neck into the matrimonial halter; we are all of us very sorry for it for we know that nothing combin'd with love, will at last make nothing at all.

I was not much surpris'd at the particulars you are pleas'd to mention about Rousseau. According to the thorough knowledge I have had of him I look on that man as a mere philosophical quack, full of affectation, of pride, of oddities and even villainies; the work he is going to publish justifies the last imputation. Is his memory so short as to forget that Mr Grimm, for those 9 years past, has taken care of the mother of his wench or *gouvernante* whom he left to starve here after having debauch'd her daughter and having got her 3 or 4 times with child. That great philosopher should remember that Mr. Grimm has in his hands letters under his own hand-writing that prove him the most ungrateful dogg in the world. During his last stay in Paris he made some attempts to see Mr Diderot, and being refused that favor, he pretended that Diderot endeavoured to see him, but that himself had refused peremptorily to comply with his request. I hope these particulars will suffice to let you know what you are to think of that illustrious man. I send you here a copy of a letter supposed to come from the King of Prussia, but done by Mr Horace Walpole, whereby you'll see that gentleman has found out his true character. But enough of that rascal who deserves not to be in Mr Hume's company but rather among the bears, if there are any in the mountains of Wales.

I am surprized you have not receiv'd yet the *Encyclopédie*, for a great number of copies have been sent over already to England unless you have left your subscription here, where hitherto not one copy has been delivered for prudent reasons. We have had in the French Comedy a new play called *Le Philosophie sans le savoir* done and acted in a new stile, quite natural and moving: it has a prodigious success and deserves it extremely well. Marmontel will give us very soon upon the Italian stage his comical opera of *La Bergère des Alpes*. I hope it will prove very agreeable to the Publick, having been very much delighted by the rehearsal of it; the music was done by Mr Cohaut who teaches my wife to play on the luth. We expect a tragedy of the Dutch Barnvelt.

Mr Wilkes is still in this town, where he intends to stay until you give him leave to return to his native country. We have had the pleasure of seeing Mr Chanquion, your friend, who seems to be a very discerning gentleman and to whom in favor of your friendship I have shown all the politeness I could. I hear that S^{r}

James Macdonald has been ill at Parma, but is now recovered and in Rome. Abbé Galliani is still at Naples and stands a fair chance of being employ'd in the ministry there.

Adieu, very dear Sir and remember your
affectionate friend
D'HOLBACH

HOLBACH TO WILKES

(Brit. Mus. Mss., Vol. 30869, p. 39)

PARIS the 22[d] of May (1766)

My dear Sir

I am extremely glad to know your lucky passage and happy arrival in your native country. I hope you know too well the sincere dispositions of my heart as to doubt of the friendship I have vowed to you for life; it has been of too long a duration to be shaken by any circumstances, and especially by those that do honor to you. I shall be very happy if your affairs (that seem to be in a fair way) permit you to drop over very soon to spend some time in this place along with Miss Wilkes to whom Mad[e] D'Holbach and I pay our best compliments. I can easily paint to my imagination the pleasure you both felt at your first meeting; everybody that has any sensibility must be acquainted with the grateful pangs in those moving circumstances.

Your case with the hawker at your entry in London is very odd and whimsical you did extremely well to humour the man in his opinion about Mr. Wilkes. I dare say if you had done otherwise his fist would have convinc'd you of the goodness of your cause, and then it would have been impossible for you to pass for a dead man any longer; which however, I think was very necessary for you in the beginning. I expect with great eagerness the settlement of your affairs with the ministry to your own satisfaction; be persuaded, Dear Sir, that nobody interests himself in your happiness than myself, and nothing will conduce more to it than your steady attachment to the principles of honor and patriotism.

If you don't find a way of disposing of the little packet, you need not take much trouble about it, and you may bring it back along with you, when you come to this place, as to the kind offers you are so good as to make me about commissions, experience has taught me that it is unsafe to trust you with them, so I beg leave with gratitude to decline your proposals as that point.

All our common friends and acquaintances desire their best compliments to you, and believe me, my dear Sir.

Your affectionate oblig'd humble servant

D'Holbach

Holbach to Wilkes

(Brit. Mus. Mss., VOL 30869, p. 81)

Paris 9ber 10th 1766

My very Dear Sir

I receiv'd with the greatest pleasure the news of your lucky arrival in Engelland. You know the sentiments of my heart, and are undoubtedly convinc'd how much I wish for the good success of all your enterprises tho I am to be a great looser by it. I rejoice very heartily at the fine prospect you have now in view and don't doubt but the persons you mention will succeed if they are in good earnest: which is allways a little doubtful in people of that Kidney.

We have had the pleasure of seeing Miss Wilkes three or four times since your departure, she is extreamly well and longs for the return of her friend Mlle Helvetius the 20th of this month.

Rousseau will very likely hate the English very cordially for making him pay so dear for his books, it is however a sign that he told us a lye when he pretended in his writings to have no books at all, as to his guitar he should buy a new one to tune his heart a little better than he did before.

We have no news here, except the Election of Mr Thomas as a member of the french academy. Marquis Beccaria is going to leave us very soon being obliged to return to Milan: Count Veri will at the same time set out for England.

I'll be oblig'd to you for a copy or two of the book printed in holland you mentioned in your letter you may send it by some private opportunity to Miss Wilkes, with, proper directions. A gentleman of our Society should be glad to get 2 copies of Baskervilles' virgil *in octavo*.

Tho Mr Davenport and Rousseau seem to be pleased very much with one another, I suppose they may very soon be tired of their squabbling, and the latter like the apostles will shake of against the barbarous Britons the dust of his feet. Receive the hearty compliments of my wife and all our friends. You know the true sentiments of my heart for you,

Dear Sir. I am with great sincerity

your most obedient humble Servant

D'HOLBACH

HOLBACH TO WILKES

(Brit. Mus. Mss., Vol. 30869, p. 173)

Dear Sir

I receiv'd with a great deal of pleasure your friendly letter from Ostende of the 26th. nov. I was extreamly glad to hear your happy arrival at that place, and do not doubt but you met with a lucky passage to Dover the following day, we are now enjoying the conversation of your British friends about elections; that will not be tedious for you if, according to your hopes, you should succeed in your projects.

I see by your letter that instead of coming back directly by Calais you intend to travel with Miss Wilkes through Antwerp and the Low countries, which I should think not very advisable in this rigorous season of the year, for generally at that time the waters are lock'd up by the frost and travelling is bad et tedious and may be would prove hurtful to your tender fellow traveler to whom my wife and I desire our best compliments. Such a scheme will be more advantagious for you both and more conformable to the wishes of your friends in this place.

I hope your arrival in London will contribute to reconcile abbé Galliani to that place, where he complains of having not heard of the sun since he set his foot on British shore, however he may comfort himself for we have had very little of it in this country. The Abbé must be overjoy'd at the news of the Jesuits being expell'd from his Native country for now he may say *Gens inimica mihi Tyrrhenum navigat aquor*. We have no material news in this country, except that the queen continues to be in a very bad state of health.

If there is some good new romance I'll be oblig'd to bring it over along with you as, well as a couple of french books call'd *Militaire philosophe* and *Théologie portative* in case you may easily find them in London, for we cannot get them here. I am told the works of one Morgan have been esteem'd in your country but I don't know the titles of them, if you should know them and meet with them with facility, I should be very much oblig'd to you provided you make me pay a little more than you have done hitherto for your commissions.

All our common friends beg their compliments and I wish for your speedy return, and I am Sincerely
Dear Sir

Your faithful affectionate humble servant

D'HOLBACH

PARIS the 10th of decemb. 1767

HOLBACH TO WILKES

(Brit. Mus. Mss., Vol. 30870, p. 59)

GRANDVAL, 17th of July 1768

Dear Sir

I receiv'd with a great deal of pleasure your very agreeable letter of the 28th of last month. I am extreamly glad that your generous soul is very far from sinking under the weight of these Misfortunes, and to see that you don't give up the hopes of carrying triumphantly your point notwithstanding the discouragements you have met with lately. I need not tell you how much your friends in Paris and I in particular interest ourselves in all the events that may befall you. Our old friendship ought to be a sure pledge of my sincere sentiments for you, and of my best wishes for your good success in all your undertakings. I believe you can do no better but to keep strictly to the rules you have laid down for your conduct, and I don't doubt but you'll find it will answer the best to your purpose.

I am very much oblig'd to you, Dear Sir, for the kind offers you make in your friendly letter. I have desir'd already Mr Suard to bring over a few books lately published in your metropolis. I am very glad to hear that Gentleman is pleas'd with his journey.

There's no possibility of getting for you a compleat sett of Callots engravings. Such a collection must be the business of many years; it is to be found only after the decease of some curious men who have taken a great deal of trouble to collect them. I found indeed in two shops 8 or 10 of them, but the proofs (les épreuves) were very indifferent and they wanted to sell them excessively dear; in general 200 guineas would procure a collection very far from being compleat. My wife and all our common acquaintence desire their best compliments to you and to Miss Wilkes and you know the sentiments wherewith I am for ever

Dear Sir

your affectionate friend and
very humble servant
D'HOLBACH

HOLBACH TO WILKES

(Brit. Mus. Mss., Vol. 30871, p. 16)

PARIS the 19th of March 1770

Dear Sir

I receiv'd with a due sense of gratitude the favour of your last letter, and was overjoy'd to hear from yourself that your long confinement has not been able hitherto to obstruct the lively flow of your spirits. A little more patience and you'll reach the end of all your misfortunes, that have been faithfully partaken by your friends in England and abroad, for my own part I wish most sincerely that everything for the future may turn to your profit and welfare, without hurting that of your country, to whom, as a lover of mankind, I am a well wisher.

My wife desires her best compliments to you and your beloved Daughter, whom we both expect to see again with a great deal of pleasure in this country next month. Notwithstanding our bad circumstances we are making very great preparations for the Wedding of the Dauphin, and our metropolis begins already to be filled with foreigners that flock hither from all parts of the world. Our friend Mr D'Alainville is to set out at the end of April to fetch the Archdutchess at Strasbourg and bring mask (ed) (?) her different stages on the road to Versailles.

We have no news in the literary world except that Voltaire is become lately *le père temporal*, that is to say the benefactor of the *Capucins du pays de Gex* where he lives, a title of which all his pranks seemd to exclude him, but grace you know, is omnipotent, and monks are not over nice when there is something to be got by their condescension.

If the hurry of affairs whould leave you any moments to read curious books I would advise you to peruse two very strange works lately publish'd viz *Recherches philosophiques sur les américains*, le *Système de la Nature* par Mirabaud. I suppose you'll find them cheaper and more easily in London that at Paris.

All your late acquaintances in this Town desire me to present you with their sincere compliments and best wishes; as to mine you know that they have no other object but your Welfare.

I am, Dear Sir, for ever

your most affectionate friend
and humble servant

D'HOLBACH

P. S. I'll be very much oblig'd to you for sending over to me in 2 vol. small octavo.

HOLBACH TO WILKES

(Wilkes, Correspondence, London, 1805, Vol. 4, p. 176)

PARIS, April 27; 1775

"*My Lord*,

"I received with the utmost gratitude your lordship's friendly letter of the 28th of March. (1775?) I should have done myself the honor of answering sooner to your kind propositions, if I had not been prevented by some gouty infirmities that have assailed in the beginning of this spring. I esteem myself very happy to find that the hurry of business, and your exhaltation to the rank of chief-magistrate, could not make you forget your friendship to me; though my present circumstances do not permit me to make use of your friendly invitation, be persuaded my very dear lord that Madame D'Holbach and myself shall forever keep these signs of your kindness, in very grateful remembrance.

We both desire our best compliments to your very amiable lady-mayoress: who acted so well her part lately in the Egyptian hall, to the satisfaction of that prodigious crowd you have been entertaining there. All members of our society that have had the happiness of being acquainted with you, desire to be kindly remembered; and a continuation of your valuable friendship shall for ever be the utmost ambition

my lord
of your most sincerely devoted
D'HOLBACH"

GALIANI TO HOLBACH

(Galiani, Corresp., Vol. I, p. 199)

NAPLES, le 21 juillet, 1770

Bonjour, mon cher Baron,

J'ai vu le *Système de la Nature*. C'est la ligne où finit la tristesse de la morne et sèche vérité, au-delà commence la gaieté du roman. Il n'y a rien de mieux que de se persuader que les dés sont pipés: cette idée en enfante milles autres, et un nouveau monde se régénère. Le M. Mirabaud est un vrai abbé Terray de la métaphysique. Il fait des réductions, des suspensions, et cause la banqueroute du savoir, du plaisir et de l'esprit humain. Mais vous allez me dire qu'aussi il y avait trop de nonvaleurs: on était trop endetté, il courait trop de papiers non réels sur la place. C'est vrai aussi, et voilà pourquoi la crise est arrivée.

Adieu, mon cher baron. Ecrivez-moi de longues lettres, pour que le plaisir en soit plus grand. Embrassez moi longuement la baronne, et soyez longue dans tout que vous faites, dans tout ce que vous patientez, dans tout ce que vous espérer. La longanimité est une belle vertu; c'est elle qui me fait espérer de revoir Paris.

Adieu.[1]

---

[1] [*Greetings, my dear Baron,*

I have seen the *System of Nature*. It's on the line where dreary sadness and dry truth end, beyond that the joy of the novel begins. There is nothing better than to be convinced that the dice are loaded: this idea begets thousands of others, and a new world is born. M. Mirabaud is a real Abbé Terray of

HOLBACH TO GALIANI

(Critica, Vol. I, 1903, p. 489)

GRANDVAL, le 25 d'août 1770

Bonjour, mon très délicieux abbé,

J'ai bien reçu votre très-précieuse lettre du 21 de juillet qui m'accuse la réception de celle que je vous avais écrite le 3 de juin. Je vois que celle-ci a été longtemps en route, attendu que M. Torcia à qui M. Diderot s'était chargé de la remettre, a encore traînassé quelque temps à Paris, suivant la louable coutume des voyageurs qui nous quittent toujours avec peine.

Je suis bien aise que vous ayez lu le livre de Mirabaud qui fait un bruit affreux dans ce pays. L'abbé Bergier l'a déjà réfuté très-longuement et sa réponse paraîtra cet hiver. La Sorbonne est, dit-on, occupée à détruire ce maudit *Système* qui lui paraît au moins hérétique. Voltaire lui-même se prépare à le pulvériser; en attendant nos seigneurs du Parlement y viennent d'y répondre par des fagots, ainsi qu'à quelque autres ouvrages de même trempe. Ce qu'il y a de fâcheux c'est que l'ouvrage de V. qui a pour titre *Dieu et les hommes* a été enveloppé dans la même condamnation, ce qui doit déplaire souverainement à l'auteur. Je me rappelle à cette occasion ce que M. Hume dit d'un catholique que Henri VIII fit conduire au bûcher avec quelques hérétiques, et dont le seul chagrin était d'être brûlé en si mauvaise compagnie. Nonobstant toutes ces réfutations, il parait tous les

---

metaphysics. He makes reductions, suspensions, and brings about the bankruptcy of knowledge, pleasure and the human spirit. But you will say to me that there are also too many worthless parts: it is too derivative, it runs together too many unreal articles. This is also true, and that is why the crisis happened.

Farewell, my dear Baron. Write me long letters, so that the pleasure will be greater. Give the Baroness a long kiss from me, and take time over everything you do, everything you wait for, everything you hope for. Forbearance is a great virtue, it's what gives me hope of seeing Paris again.

Farewell.]

jours quelques nouveaux ouvrages impies, au point que je suis très surpris que la récolte ait été si bonne dans le royaume. En dernier lieu on vient de publier un ouvrage sous le titre de *Droit des souverains sur les biens du clergé*, qui, sans contenir des impiétés n'en est pas moins déplaisant pour cela: Il va droit à la cuisine, et veut que pour liquider la dette nationale on vende tous les biens ecclésiastiques et que l'on met nos pontifes à la pension. Vous sentez qu'une proposition si mal sonnante n'a pu manquer de mettre le ciel en courroux; sa colère s'est déchargé sur cinq ou six libraires et colporteurs qui ont été mis en prison.[2]

---

[2] [*Greetings, my most delightful Abbé,*

I received your most precious letter of 21 July which tells me that you have received the one I wrote on 3 June. I see that it took a long time to get there, as Mr. Torcia, who was asked by M. Diderot to deliver it, was detained some time in Paris, according to the praiseworthy custom of travelers who always leave us in pain.

I am glad that you have read Mirabaud's book which has made such a terrible stink in this country. Abbé Bergier has already refuted it at great length and his response will be published this winter. The Sorbonne is, allegedly, set to destroy this accursed *System* which appears heretical to it, at the very least. Voltaire himself is preparing to pulverize it; in the meantime, our Parliamentary masters will just respond with faggots, and some other works of the same stamp. What is unfortunate is that the V.'s work,which is entitled *God and Man,* has been caught up in the same condemnation, which must royally displease the author. I remember M. Hume describing a Catholic who, on being sent to the stake with some heretics by Henry VIII, said his only regret was being burned in such bad company. Notwithstanding all these rebuttals, new impious works appear every day, to the extent that I'm very surprised that the harvest has been so good in the kingdom. Finally a book has just been published under the title of *the Right of Sovereigns over Clergy Property*, which although it contains no impiety, is no less unpalatable for it: it goes right to the nub, and aims to liquidate the national debt by selling off all church property and putting our pontiffs out to grass. You might think that such an evil-sounding proposal couldn't fail to enrage heaven; its anger has fallen on five or six booksellers and hawkers who have been imprisoned.]

Bibliography. Part I. Editions of Holbach's Works in Chronological Order.

As the works of Holbach are not yet cataloged in the Bibliothèque Nationale, the following list is doubtless incomplete. The numbers given are those of the Bibliothèque Nationale and the British Museum where the books were used, except in cases where they were available in Boston, New York or Washington.

Abbreviations

B. N., Bibliothèque Nationale.
B. M., British Museum.
L. C., Library of Congress.
C. U., Columbia University.
H. U., Harvard University.
U. T. S., Union Theological Seminary.
G. T. S., General Theological Seminary.
A. T. S., Andover Theological Seminary.
N. Y., New York Public Library.
B. P., Boston Public Library.

Of about 120 editions consulted, C. U. had 13; U. T. S. 7; N. Y. 7; H. U. 6; B. P. 5; L. C. 4; A. T. S. 3; G. T. S. I. There are 20 or more editions in existence that were not to be found in the library catalogs consulted.

1752. Lettre à une dame d'un certain âge sur l'état présent de l'Opéra. En Arcadie aux dépens de l'Académie Royale

de Musique, (Paris, 8vo, pp. 11.)
B. M. 1103 b 21 (2).

1752. Arrêt rendu à l'amphithéâtre de l'Opéra, sur la plainte du milieu du parterre intervenant dans la querelle des deux coins. (Paris, 1752, 8vo, pp. 16.)
B. N. Yf 7726 (attributed to Diderot).

1752. Art de la Verrerie, De Neri, Merret et Kunckel; auquel on a ajouté Le *Sol Sine Veste* D'Orschall; *L'Helioscopium videndi sine veste solem Chymicum*; Le *Sol Non Sine Veste*: Le Chapitre XI du *Flora Saturnizans* de Henckel, Sur la Vitrification des Végétaux : Un Mémoire sur la manière de faire le Saffre; Le Secret des vraies Porcelaines de la Chine et de Saxe; Ouvrages où l'on trouvera la manière de faire le Verre et le Crystal, d'y porter des Couleurs, d'imiter les Pierres Précieuses, de préparer et colorer les Emaux, de faire la Potasse, de peindre sur le Verre, de préparer des Vernis, de composer de Couvertes pour des Fayances et Poteries, d'extraire la Couleur Pourpre de l'Or, de contrefaire les Rubis, de faire le Soffre, de faire et peindre les Porcelaines, etc. Traduits de l'Allemand Par M. D... A Paris Durand, rue St. Jacques, au Griffon. Pissot, Quai des Augustins, à la Sagesse. Avec Approbation et Privilège du Roi (in quarto).
B. N. V. 11028.
C. U. A. n H 35 (Avery Library).

1753. Minéralogie, ou description générale des substances du règne minéral. Par Mr. Jean Gotshalk Wallerius, Professeur Royale de Chymie, de Métallurgie et de Pharmacie dans l'Université d'Upsal, de l'Académie de l'Allemand, A Paris, Chez Durand, rue S. Jacques, au Griffon.Impériale des Curieux de la Nature. Ouvrage traduit Pissot, Quai de Conti, à la Croix d'Or, MDCCLII. Avec Approbation et Privilège du Roi (2 vols., 8vo, pp. xlvii + 569 + 284). Followed by (second title page) Hydrologie, ou description du règne aquatique, divisés par classes, gendres, espèces et variétés, avec la manière de faire l'essai des eaux (256 p.).

B. N., S. 1992 (2).

B. M. 987 h. 9-10.

—. Ibid. (Paris, Herissant, Durand, 1759, 2 vols., 8vo.) N. Y., P. W. D.

H. U. Geol. 7257-59.

B. M. 970 h.l.

1756. Introduction à la Minéralogie; ou connoissance des eaux, des sucs terrestres, des sels, des terres, des pierres, des minéraux, et des métaux: avec une description abrégée des opérations de métallurgie. Ouvrage posthume de M. J. F. Henckel, publié sous le titre de *Henckelius in Mineralogiâ redivivus* et traduit de l'Allemand. A Paris, Chez Guillaume Cavelier, Libraire, rue S. Jacques, au Lys d'Or. MDCCLVI. Avec Approbation et Privilège du Roi. (2 vols., 12vo, pp. lxxi + 204 + 371.)

B. N. 19930 (1).

1758. Chimie métallurgique, Dans laquelle on trouvera la Théorie et la Pratique de cet Art. Avec des Experiences sur la Densité des Alliages des Métaux, et des demi-Métaux; et un Abrégé de Docimastique. Avec Figures. Par M. C. E. Gellert, Conseiller des Mines de Saxe et de l'Académie Imperiale de Petersbourg. Ouvrages traduits de l'Allemand. A Paris, Chez Briasson, rue Saint Jacques; Avec Approbation et Privelège. (2 vols., 12mo, pp. xii + 296 + xvii + 351.)

B. N., R. 37032 (3).

1759. Traités de physique, d'histoire naturelle, de minéralogie et de métallurgie. (Paris, 1759, 3 vols., 12mo.) (General title.)

Tome I. L'Art des Mines, ou Introduction aux

connoissances nécessaires pour l'exploitation des mines métalliques avec un traité des exhalaisons minérales ou moufettes, et plusieurs mémoires sur differens sujets d'Histoire Naturelle-Avec figures. Par M. Jean Gotlob Lehmann, Docteur en Médecine, Conseiller des Mines de Sa Majesté Prussienne, de l'Académie Royale des Sciences de Berlin et de celle des Sciences utiles de Mayence Traduit de l'Allemand. A Paris, Chez Jean Thomas Herrisant MDCCLIX. Avec Approbation et Privilège du Roi.

Tome II. Traité de la formation des métaux et de leurs matrices ou minières, ouvrage fondé sur les principes de la physique et de la minéralogie et confirmé par des expériences chymiques. Par M. J. G. Lehmann, etc. Traduit de l'Allemand.

Tome III. Essai d'une Histoire Naturelle des couches de la terre. Dans lequel on traite de leur formation, de leur situation, des minéraux, des métaux et des fossiles qu'elles contiennent. Avec des considerations physiques sur les causes des Tremblements de Terre et de leur propagation. Ouvrages traduits de l'Allemand, et augmentés de Notes du Traducteur etc.

H. U., M, Z.

B. M. 990 c. 16-18.

1759. Les plaisirs de l'imagination, poème en trois chants, par M. Akenside. Traduit de l'anglais. A Amsterdam, Arkstée et Merkus, et se trouve à Paris chez Pissot, Quai de Conti MDCCLIX (8vo).

B. N. 2 ex. Yk 2362 et 2498.

B. M. 1162 f 20.

—. Ibid. Les plaisirs de l'imagination, poème en trois chants, Par Akenside, traduit de l'Anglais par le baron d'Holbach, augmenté de Notes historiques et littéraires, de la vie de l'auteur et du Traducteur, par Pissot. Paris, Hubert MDCCCVI (1806-18vo).

B. N. Yk 2363.

B. M. 1065 b 20 (2).

1760. Pyritologie, ou Histoire Naturelle de la Pyrite, ouvrage dans lequel on examine l'origine, la nature, les propriétés et les usages de ce Minéral important, et de la plupart des autres Substances du même Règne: on y a joint le Flora Saturnisans où L'Auteur dèmontre l'Alliance qui se trouve entre les Végétaux et les Minéraux; et les Orpuscules Minéralogiques, Qui comprennent un Traité de l'Appropriation, un Traité de L'Origine des Pierres, plusieurs Mémoires sur la Chymie et l'Histoire Naturelle, avec un Traité des Maladies des Mineurs et des Fondeurs. Par M. Jean-Frederic Henkel, Docteur en Médicine, Conseiller des Mines du Roi de Pologne, Electeur de Saxe; de l'Académie Imperiale des Curieux de la Nature et de celle de Berlin. Ouvrages Traduit de l'Allemand [by Baron d'Holbach and M., Charas] à Paris, Chez jean Thomas Hérissant, Libraire, Rue S. Jacques, à S. Paul et à S. Hilaire. MDCCLX. Avec Approbation et Privilège du Roi. (Paris, 1760, quarto, pp. xvi + 524.)

B. N. 5324.

B. M. 34 c 15.

1760. Oeuvres Métallurgiques de M. Jean-Christian Orschall, Inspecteur des Mines de S. A. S. le Land-grave de Hesse-Cassel. Contenant I. L'Art de la Fonderie; II. Un Traité de la Siquation; III. Le Traité de la Macération des Mines; IV. Le Traité des Trois Merveilles; (Traduit de l'Allemand) Le prix est de 50 sols broché et de 3 liv. relié. A Paris, Chez Hardy, Libraire, rue S. Jacques au dessus de celle de la Parcheminerie à la Colonne d'Or. MDCCLX. Avec Approbation et Privilège du Roi. (12mo, pp. + 394.)

B. N., S 19,992.

1764. Recueil des mémoires les plus intéressants de chymie, et d'histoire naturelle, contenus dans les actes de l'Académie d'Upsal, et dans les Mémoires de l'Académie Royale des Sciences de Stockholm; Publiés depuis1720 jusqu'en 1760. Pierre-Fr. Didot, le jeune, Quai des Augustins, à S. Augustin. MDCCLXIV. Avec Approbation et Privilège du Roi. (2 vols., 12mo, pp. viii + 687.)

B. N. R 15483 (4).

1765. Histoire du règne de la Reine Anne d'Angleterre, contenant Les Négociations de la paix d'Utrecht, et les démêlés qu'elle occasionna en Angleterre. Ouvrage posthume du Docteur Jonathan Swift. Doyen de S. Patrice en Irelande: Publié sur un Manuscrit corrigé de la propre main de l'Auteur, et traduit de l'Anglais par M... [d'Holbach and Eidous]. A Amsterdam, Chez Marc-Michel Rey, et Arkstée et Merkus. MDCCLXV. (12mo, pp. xxiv + 416.)

B. N. 8vo Nc 1718.

1766. Traité du Soufre, ou Remarques sur la dispute qui s'est élevée entre les chymistes, au sujet du Soufre, tant commun, combustible ou volatil, que fixe, etc. Traduit de l'Allemand de Stahl. A Paris, Chez Pierre-Francois Didot, le jeune. Quai de Augustins à Saint-Augustin. MDCCLXVI. Avec Approbation et Privilège du Roi. (12mo, pp. 392.)

B. N., R 51709.

B. M. 233 b 15.

1766. L'Antiquité dévoilée par ses usages, ou Examen critique des principales Opinions, Cérémonies et Institutions réligieuses et politiques des différens Peuples de la Terre. Par feu M., Boulanger. Homo, quod rationis est particeps, consequentiam cernit causas rerum videt, earumque progressus et quasi antecessiones non ignorat, similitudines compare, rebus praesentibus adjungit at anectit futuras. —Cicero, De Offic. Lib. I. C. 4. A

Amsterdam, Chez Marc-Michel Rey, MDCCLXVI. (Quarto pp. viii + 412.)

B. N., E 690.

C. U., A P. B 66 (Avery Library).

—. Ibid. (1766, 3 vols., 12mo.)

B. N. *E 2446-2448.

—. Ibid. (1772, 3 Vols., (12mo.)

B. N. *E 2445 (VIII).

B. M. 4506 a 1.

—. Ibid. (Amsterdam, 1777, 3 vols., 12mo, pp. lx + 355 + 391 + 396.)

B. M. 696 b 35.

—. Ibid. In Oeuvres de Boulanger T. I-IV En Suisse. De l'Imprimerie Philosophique MDCCXCI. (4 vols., (12mo.)

B. N., Z 24316-24319.

—. Ibid. In *Oeuvres de Boulanger* T. I-II Amsterdam. (Paris, 2 vols., 8vo.) (Quérard.)

1767. Le Christianisme dévoilé, ou Examen des principes et des effets de la religion Chrétienne. Par feu M. Boulanger. Superstitio error infanus est, amandos timet, quos colit violat; quid enim interest, utrum Deos neges, an infames? Senec. Ep. 12. A Londres, MDCCLVI (Nancy, Leclerc, 1761, 8vo, pp. xxviii + 295).

B. N., D2 5305.

B. M. 4016 bb 6.

B. M., C 2863 (another copy with MS. notes by Voltaire).

—. Ibid. (Londres, 1767, 8vo, pp. xx + 236.) Printed at John Wilkes' private press in George St. Westminster, according to MS. note in title page.

B. M. 4017 de. 13.

—. Ibid. (Londres, 1767, 8vo, pp. 244.)

A. T. S. 6 11.

—. Ibid. (A Paris, Chez les Libraires Associés, 1767, 8vo, pp. xvii + 218.)

B. N., D2 8364.

—. Ibid. (Londres [Amsterdam], 1767, 12mo.)

B. M. 696 b 34

—. Ibid. Oeuvres de Boulanger T. VII. (En Suisse de l'Imprimerie philosophique, 1791, 12mo.)

B. N., Z 23421.

—. Ibid. Oeuvres de Boulanger T. V, 1793.

—. Christianity Unveiled; being an examination of the principles and effects of the Christian Religion, from the French of Boulanger, Author of *Researches into the Origin of Oriental Despotism*, by W. M. Johnson. New York, 1795, printed at the Columbian Press by Robertson and Gowan for the editor and sold by the principal book sellers in the United States. (12mo, pp. ix + 238.)

B. M. 4017 de 4.

B. M. 900 i. 1, (7) another copy with MS. Notes.

B. P.... 7490 a 22.

—. Ibid. London, printed and published by R. Carlile, 55 Fleet St. 1819 (8vo, pp. 98.)

B. M. 4016 d. 13.

—. Ibid. The Deist, etc. Vol. II, published by R. Carlile, 1819. (8vo, pp. vii + 125.)

B. M. 4015 f 11.

—. El Cristianismo a descurbierto, ó examen de los principios y efectos de la religion cristiana. Escrito en Francés por Boulanger y traducido al castellano por S. D. V.... Londres en la emprenta de Davidson, 1821. (12mo, pp. xxvi + 246.)

B. M. 4016 df 6.

1767. L'Esprit du clergé, ou Le Christianisme primitif vengé des entreprises et des excès de nos Prêtres modernes.

Traduit de l'Anglois à Londres (Amsterdam) MDCCLXVII (2 vols. 8vo, pp. 2 + 10 + 240).

B. M. pp. 54.

1767. De l'imposture sacerdotale, ou Recueil de Pièces sur le Clergé. Traduites de l'Anglois. Londres (Amsterdam) MDCCLXVII. (12mo, pp. 144.)

B. N., D2 8368 (7).

Contains, Tableau fidèle des papes. *Traduit d'une Brochure Anglaise* de M. Davisson, Publie sous le titre de *a true picture of Popery*, pp. 1-35.

De l'insolence pontificale, ou des Prétentions ridicules du Pape et des Flatteurs de la Cour de Rome. *Extrait de la Profession de Foi du célèbre Giannone*, par. M. Davisson, pp. 36-54.

Sermon. Sur les fourberies et les impostures du Clergé Romain, *Traduit de l'Anglois sur une Brochure publiée à Londres en 1735* par M. Bourn Birmingham, Sous le titre de *Popery a Craft*, pp. 55-84.

Le Prêtrianisme opposé au Christianisme. Ou la Religion des Prêtres comparée à celle de Jésus-Christ, ou examen de la différence qui se trouve entre les Apôtres et les Membres du Clergé moderne. *Publié en Anglois en 1720 sous le titre de* Priestanity. Or a View of the disparity between the Apostles and the Modern Clergy, pp. 85-108.

Des Dangers de l'Eglise, *Traduit de Anglois sur une Brochure Publiée eu 1719*. Par M., Thomas Gordon, Sous le titre d'*Apology for the danger of the Church*, etc., pp. 109-128.

Le Simbole d'un Laïque, ou Profession de Foi d'un homme désintéressé. Traduit de l'Anglois de M. Gordon, Sur une brochure publiée en 1720. Sous le titre de *the creed of anindependent Whig*, pp. 129-144.

—. Ibid. Published under title De La Monstruosité pontificale, ou Tableau fidèle des Papes. *Traduit de l'Anglois* Londres MDCCLXXII. (16vo, pp. 55.)

B. N., H. 19859.

1768. Examen des Prophéties qui servent de fondement à la religion chrétienne, avec un Essai de critique sur les Prophètes et les Prophéties en général. Ouvrages traduits de l'Anglois. Londres MDCCLXVIII. (8vo, pp. 234.)

B. N., D2 5190.

B. M. 4017 de 18.

Contains, Discours sur les fondements de la religion chrétienne, pp. 1-111.

Extrait De l'Ouvrage qui a pour titre: Examen du Septème de ceux qui prétendent que les Prophéties se sont accomplies à la lettre. The Scheme of literal Prophecy considered, etc., 1727. (8vo, pp. 118-234.)

1768. David, ou l'Histoire de l'homme selon le coeur de Dieu, ouvrage traduit de l'Anglois. Saül, et David, tragédie en 5 actes d'après l'Anglois.... (Londres, 1768, 8vo.)

B. N. 3 ex. LD2 5194, Hz 1542, et Rès Z. Beuchot 798 (2).

B. M. 4014 a 67 (1).

1768. Lcs Prêtres démasqués, ou des iniquités du clergé chrétien. Ouvrage traduit de l'Anglois. Londres. MDCCLXVIII. (16vo, pp. 180.)

B. N., D2 4639.

B. M. 4017 de 29.

1768. Lettres philosophiques, sur l'origine des Préjugés, du Dogme de l'Immortalité de l'Ame, de l'Idolâtrie et de la Superstition; sur le Système de Spinoza et sur l'origine du mouvement dans la matière. Traduites de l'Anglois de J. Toland. Opinionum commenta delet dies, naturae judicia confirmat. Cicero, de Nat. Deor. lib. II. A Londres (Amsterdam). 1768. MDCCLXVIII. (8vo, pp. 267.)

B. N., D2 5203.

B. M. 4015 de 48.

Containing, Préface ou Lettre à un ami, en lui

envoyant les Dissertations suivantes, dans laquelle l'Auteur rend compte des motifs qui les ont fait écrire. (pp. 12-26.)

Première Lettre. De L'origine et de la Force de ces Préjugés. (pp. 27-44.)

Seconde Lettre. Histoire du dogme de l'Immortalité de l'Ame Chez les Payens. (pp. 45-93.)

Troisième Lettre. Sur l'origine de l'Idolâtrie et sur les fondements de la Religion Payenne. (pp. 94-152.)

Quartrième Lettre. A un Gentilhomme Hollandois pour lui prouver que le système de Spinoza est dépourvu de fondements et pèche dans ses principes. (pp. 154-186.)

Cinquième Lettre. Dans laquelle on prouve que le mouvement est essentiel à la Matière; en réponse à quelques remarques qui ont été faites à l'Auteur au sujet de sa réfutation du Système de Spinoza.

Nunc quae mobilitas fit reddita Materiaë Corporibus paucis licet hinc cognoscere, Memmi. Lucret., lib. II, vers 142. (pp. 187-267.)

1768. Théologie portative, ou Dictionnaire Abrégé de la Religion Chrétienne. Par Mr. l'Abbé Bernier, Licencié en Théologie. Audite hoc Sacerdotes, et attendite Domus Israël, et Domus Regis auscultate; quia vobis Judicium est, quoniam Laquens facti estis Speculationi et rete expansum super Thabor. Osée, Chap. V, Vers. I. Londres (Amsterdam), MDCCLXVIII (1767), (12mo, pp. 243).

B. N., D2 14334

B. M. 703 a 25.

—. Ibid. Londres (Suisse), 1768.

—. Ibid. A Rome, MDCCLXXV (8vo, pp. 213).

B. N., D2 8370.

—. Ibid. Augmentée d'un Volume. A Rome, avec permission et privilège du Conclave. (2 vols., 12mo

(1776).)

B. N., D2 8371.

—. Ibid. Under title. Manuel Théologique, en form de Dictionnaire. Ouvrage très utile aux personnes des deux sexes pour le salut de leurs âmes, par l'abbé Bernier etc. Rome, 1785 Au Vatican de l'Imprimerie du Conclave. (2 vols., 8vo.)

—. Ibid. 1802.

1768. Le Militaire philosophe, ou Difficultés sur la Religion, proposées au R. P. Malebranche, Prêtre de l'Oratoire. Par un ancien Officier. Londres (Amsterdam) MDCCLXVIII. (8vo, pp. 193.)

C. U. 201 N 14.

—. Ibid. 1770 (8vo).

B. M. 4015 bb 32.

—. Ibid. 1776 (8vo).

B. M. 4015 de 34.

(Last chapter by d'Holbach.)

1768. La Contagion sacrée, ou Histoire Naturelle de la Superstition. Ouvrage traduit dc l'Anglois. *Prima mali labes*. Londres(Amsterdam), MDCCLXVII. (2 vols. in 1, 8vo.)

B. N., D2 5195.

C. U. 194 H 69 P.

—. Ibid. Avec des notes relatives aux Circonstances. Nouvelle Edition. A Paris, de l'Imprimerie de Lemaire, rue d'Enfer no. 141, An 5 de la Republique (1797). (2 vols. in 1, 8vo, pp. 179-190.)

U. T. S. 441

B. H. 723 C.

—. El Contagion sagrado, ó Historia natural de la supersticion. Paris, Rodriguez, 1822. (2 vols., 8vo.) (Quérard.)

1768. Lettres à Eugénia, ou Préservatif contre les préjugés...

arctis Relligionum animos nodis exsolvere pergo.— Lucret. de rer. nat., Lib. 4, v. 6-7. A Londres, MDCCLXVIII. (2 vols., 8vo, pp. xii + 188 + 167)

—. Ibid. Oeuvres de Nicolas Fréret, T. I, pp. 1-359. Paris, 1792. (8vo.) H. U. 19-30, vol. I.

—. Cartas á Eugenia, por Mr. Freret. Paris. Imprenta de F. Didot, 1810 (8vo, pp. viii + 358).
B. M. 4015 de 23.

—. Letters to Eugenia on the absurd, contradictory and demoralizing Dogmas and Mysteries of the Christian Religion. Now first translated from the French of Fréret, but supposed to be written by Baron Holbach, author of the System of Nature, Christianity Unveiled, Common Sense, Universal Morality, Natural Morality. R. Carlile, The Deist, etc., Vol. II, 1819, etc. (8vo, pp. 185.)
B. M. 4015 f. 11.

—. Cartas à Eugenia. Madrid, 1823, por Don Benito Cano. 2v.
N. Y., Z F F.

—. Letters to Eugenia on the absurd, contradictory and demoralizing Dogmas and Mysteries of the Christian Religion, by Baron d'Holbach, New York, published by H. M. Dubecquet, No. 190 William Street, 1833. (12vo, pp. 236.)
U. T. S. 326 B.

—. Letters to Eugenia etc., translated by Anthony C. Middleton, M.D. Boston, Josiah P. Mendum, 1857.
B. P. 5484 2.

1769. De la Cruauté religieuse. A Londres, MDCCLXIX. (16vo, pp. 228.)
B. N., D2 8365.
B. M. 4017 aa 25.
U. T. S. H 723.

—. Ibid. Amsterdam, 1775, 12vo.

1769. Le la Tolérance dans la Religion, ou de la Liberté de conscience par Crellius. L'Intolérance convaincue de crime et de folie. Ouvrage traduit de l'Anglois, Londres, MDCCLXIX. (12vo, pp. 174.)

Contains De la Tolérance dans la religion, ou de la liberté de conscience (Crellius).

De l'Intolérance dans la Religion (d'Holbach), p. 88.

Enfer détruit ou Examen Raisonné du Dogme de l'Eternité des peines. Ouvrages, tr. de L'Anglois à Londres, MDCCLXIX, p. 1.

Dissertation critique sur les tourmens de l'enfer. Traduit de L'Anglois, p. 96 (by Whitefoot).

B. N., D2 5154.

—. Ibid. Hell destroyed! Now first translated from the French of d'Alembert without any mutilations. London. Printed and published by J. W. Trust, 126 Newgate St., 1823. (8vo, pp. 47.) (Followed by Whitefoot's Torments of Hell, "now first translated from the French," to p. 83.)

1770. L'Esprit du judaïsme, ou Examen raisonné de la Loi de Moyse, et de son influence sur la Religion Chrétienne.

Atque utinam nunquam Judaea sub acta fuisset Pompeii bellis, imperioque Titi.

Latius excisae pestes contagie serpunt, Victoresques suos natio victa premit. Rutilius, Itinerar. Lia I, vs. 394, Londres, MDCCLXX. (12mo, pp. xxii + 201.)

B. N., D2 5191.

B. M. 4034 bb 38.

1770. Examen critique de la vie et des ouvrages de saint Paul, Avec une dissertation sur saint Pierre par feu M. Boulanger. Londres, 1770 (8vo), (by Peter Annet).

B. N. 3ex. [D2 5349 (2) 8367 et H. 7551].

B. M. 48o8 aa 7.

—. Ibid. Nouvelle Edition, Londres, 1790. (8vo.)

B. N. [H 13032].

—. Critical Examination of the Life of St. Paul. Translated from the French of Boulanger. "Paul, thou art beside thyself, much learning doth make thee mad." Acts, chap, 26, v 24. London. Printed and published by R. Carlile, 5 Water Lane, Fleet St., 1823. (8vo, pp. 72.)

B. M. 4372 h g (4).

1770. Histoire critique de Jésus-Christ, ou Analyse raisonnée des Evangiles. Ecce Homo. Pudet me humani generis, cuius mentis et aures talia ferre potuerunt. S. Augustin. (No date [Amsterdam, 1770?], 16mo, pp. viii + xxxii + 298.)

B. N, 7,549.

B. M. 4017 a. 45.

U. T. S. 465 H 723.

—. Ecce Homo! or a critical enquiry into the history of Jesus Christ, being a Rational Analysis of the Gospels. Edinburg, 1799.

—. Ecce Homo! or a critical enquiry into the history of Jesus Christ, being a Rational Analysis of the Gospels. (2d ed.) London, 1813. Printed, published and sold by D. I. Easton.

G. T. S. 232 G. H. 69.

—. Historia critica de Jesus Christo, o anáilisis razonado le los evangelios. Traducida del Frances, por el P. F. de T, ex-jesuita. Ecce Homo. Vel. aqui el hombre. S. Juan, cap. 19, v. 5. Londres, en la imprenta de Davidson, 1822. (2 vols., 12mo, pp. xiii + 200 + 280.)

Contains Advertencia del Traductor.

1770. Tableau des Saints, ou examen de l'esprit, de la conduite, des maximes, et du mérite des personnages que le Christianisme révère et propose pour modèles.

Hoc admonere simplices etiam potest,
Opinione alterius ne quid ponderent;
Ambitio namque diffidens mortalium

Aut gratiae subscribunt, aut odio suo;
Erit ille nottis, quem per te cognoveris.

Phaed., Lib. III, Fab. 10.

A Londres, MDCCLXX. (2 Vols., 12mo, pp. xxviii + 280 + 286.)

B. N., H 7,552.

B. M. 4,824 a a a a 27.

1770. Recueil philosophique, ou Mélange de Pièces sur la Religion et la Morale. Par différents Auteurs (ed. Naigeon).

Ovando enim ista observans quieto et libero animo esse poteris, ut ad vem gerendam non Superstionem habeas, sed Rationem ducem. —Cicero, de Divinat., Lib. 2. Londres, MDCCLXX. (2 vols., 12mo.)

B. N., D2 5309.

Vol. I, p. 129 (VI), Réflexions sur les Craintes de la Mort.

Vol. II, p. 34 (IX), Dissertation sur l'Immortalité de l'âme. Traduite de l'Anglais.

Vol. II, p. 50 (X), Dissertation sur le suicide. Traduit de l'Anglais.

Vol. II, p. 70 (XI). Problème important. La Religion est elle nécessaire à la Morale et utile à la Politique? Par M. Mirabaud.

Vol. II, p. 125 (XIII). Extrait d'un Ecrit Anglais qui a pour titre *le christianisme aussi ancien que le monde*.

1770. Essai sur les préjugés, ou, De l'influence des opinions sur les moeurs et sur le bonheur des hommes. Ouvrage contenant l'apologie de la philosophie par Mr. D. M.

Assiduite quotidiana et consuetudine oculorum assuescunt animi, neque admirantur, neque requerunt rationes earum rerum quas vident. —Cicero de Nat. Deorum, Lib. II. Londres, MDCCLXX. (8vo, pp. 394.)

B. N., R 20 553.

B. M. 8463 b b b 16.

H. U. Phil. 264840.

—. Ibid. Paris Desray an 1 (1792). (2 vols., 8vo, Cortina.)

—. Ibid. Oeuvres de Dumarsais. Paris, Pougin, 1797.T. VI8vo, pp. 43-352.

B. N., Z 23766-72.

H. U. 9578 13 VI.

—. Ibid. Paris, Niogret, 1822.

C. U. 3045 D 89.

—. Essayo sobre las preocupaciones ó del influjo de las opiniones en las costumbres y felicidad de las hombres. Por Dumarsais. En Paris. Hallase en la casa de Rosa, Librero. Gran pacio del Palacio Real. 1823. (8vo, pp. 391.)

B. N., R 34,366.

—. (Bibliothèque Nationale. Collection des meilleurs auteurs anciens et modernes.) Dumarsais. Essai sur les Préjugés. Précédé d'un Discours préliminaire et d'un Précis historique de la vie de Dumarsais par le citoyen Daube. Paris. Librairie de Bibliothèque Nationale. Rue de Richelieu 8, Près le Théâtre Francais. Ci-devant rue de Valois 1886. Tous droits resérvés (25 centimes).

B. N. 8vo R. 15952.

1770. Système de la Nature, ou Des Loix du Monde Physique et du Monde Moral. Par M. Mirabaud, Secrétaire Perpétuel et l'un des Quarante de l'Académie Française.

Natura rerum vis atque majestas in omnibus momentis fide caret, si quis modè partes ejus, ac non totam complectatur animo.—Plin. Hist., Lib. VII. Londres, MDCCLXX. (2 vols., 8vo, pp. 370 + 412.)

B. M. 4017 f 32

U. T. S. 321 H 7235.

—. Ibid, Londres, MDCCLXX. (Second edition, 2 Vols., in 8vo, pp. 366 + 408.)

B. M., D2 5166-5167.

Contains Discours préliminaire de l'Auteur (pp. 16). Avis de l'Editeur. Préface de l'Auteur, etc.

—. Abrégé du Code de la Nature, par M., Mirabaud, Secrétaire Perpétuel et l'un des Quarante de l'Académe Française. Londres. MDCCLXX. (8vo, 16 p.)

—. Ibid. Nouvelle Édition augmentée par l'auteur à laquelle on a joint plusieurs pièces des meilleurs Auteurs relatives aux mêmes objets, etc. (Ed. Naigeon.) Londres, MDCCLXXI. (2 vols. in 8vo, pp. 397-500.)

Contains Vol. II, p. 455, Réquisitoire, sur lequel est intervenu l'Arrêt du Parlement du 18 Août 1770 qui condamne à être brûlés, differens Livres ou Brochures, intitulés.

1. La Contagion sacrée...
2. Dieu et les hommes.
3. Discours sur les Miracles.
4. Examen des Apologistes.
5. Examen impartial des principales religions du Monde.
6. Christianisme dévoilé.
7. Système de la Nature.

Imprimé par ordre exprès du Roi.

B. M., D2 5168.

Reprinted in 1774, 1775-1777.

—. Ibid. Nouvelle Édition. Londres, 1780, 8vo, pp. xii + 371 + 464.

Contains *Sentiments de Voltaire sur le Système de la Nature*. Séguier's *Réquisitoire* and Holbach's *Réplique*.

B. M. 528 1. 2526.

—. Ibid. Nouvelle Édition. (2 vols. in 8vo, pp. 316 + 385.) Londres, 1781.

B. N., D2 516g.

—. Ibid. German Translation, Schreiter. Leipzig and Frankfort, 1783.

—. Ibid. Paris, An. III (1795). (3 vols. in 8vo.)

—.. The System of Nature. Translated from the French of M. Mirabeau London, 1797. Printed for G. Kearsley.

L. of C. B 2053-S G E-12 11-15959.

—. Ibid. Philadelphia, 1808. Pub. by R. Benson.

L. of C., B 2053-S G 3 E 13-11-1595 G.

—. Nature and Her Laws, as Applicable to the Happiness of Man Living in Society, Contrasted with Superstitions and Imaginary Systems. Done from the French of M. Mirabaud. London in 1816. W. Hodgson.

C. U. 194 H 69 S.

L. of C., B 2053 S g 3 E 14-11.15960

—. Système de la Nature,... Avec notes de Diderot. Nouvelle édition. Ed. Lemonnier, Paris, 1820. B. Roquefort. (2 vols. in 8vo.)

—. The System of Nature, or the Laws of the Moral and Physical World. Translated by Samuel Wilkinson from the original French of M. Mirabaud. Printed and published by Thomas Davison. (Vols. 2, 3, R. Helder, 1821). London, 1820. 3 vols in 8vo, pp. xi + 348-311-273.) Contains Life of Mirabaud, Vol. 3, pp. 263-273.

B. M. 804. de 20?

U. S. 321. H 723.

—. Système de la Nature... par le Baron d'Holbach. Nouvelle Edition avec des notes et des corrections par Diderot. Paris, Etienne Ledoux, 1821. (2 vols. in 8vo, pp. xvi + 507 +502.)

B. N., D2 5170.

B. M. 124 9 i. 26.

C. U, 194 H 69. R.

N. Y., Y C O.

Contains extract of Grimm's Literary Correspondence, Aug. 10, 1789.

—. Système de la Nature, ou des lois du monde physique et du monde morale, par le Baron d'Holbach. Nouvelle

Édition avec des notes et des corrections par Diderot etc. Paris, Domère, 1822. (4 vols. in 12mo.)

Contains Avis de Naigion. Avertissement du nouvel éditeur, pp. 11-29. Pièces diverses, pp. 30-46.

—. Sistema de la Naturaleza, con notas y correcciones por Diderot; trad, al castell. por F. A. F.... Paris, Masson hijo, 1822, 4 vols. in 18mo.

B. N., D2 5172.

—. Selections from Mirabaud's System of Nature in the Law of Reason, etc. London, 1831. (16mo, pp. 231.) Selections from Bon-Sens, pp. 39-81, 82-112.

B. M. 1387. b. 3.

—. Nature and her Laws, as Applicable to the Happiness of Man Living in Society, Contrasted with Superstitions and Imaginary Systems. From the French of M. de Mirabaud. James Watson. London, 1834. (2 vols. in 12mo, pp. xxiv + 287 + 320.) Sold for 7 s. 6 d.

B. M. 1133 b 29.

Contains

1. Publisher's Preface (by James Watson).

2. Preface.

3. A short account of the life and writings of the Baron d'Holbach(by Julian Hibbert).

—. System of Nature, new and improved edition with notes by Diderot. Translated by H. D. Robinson. New York, 1835, published by Matsell.

N. Y., Y B X.

—. System of Nature, or the laws of the moral and physical world, from the French of M. Mirabaud. (New edition, pp. 8 + 520.) London, 1840.

C. U. 194 H 69. R 1.

—. System der Natur von Mirabaud. Deutsch bearbeitet und mit Anmerkungen versehen von Biedermann. Leipzig, 1841. (8vo, pp. 604.) Georg. Wigands Verlag. T. S.

(Andover 23).

—. System der Natur.... Translated by Schreiter, 1843.

—. System of Nature, new and improved edition with notes by Diderot, translated by H. D. Robinson. Stereotype edition, Boston, 1848, in 8vo. Published by J. P. Mendum.

B. P. 00.80-6105.5.

—. System der Natur..., tr. Allhusen, 1851.

—. System of Nature..., tr. Robinson, Boston. 1853. Published by J. P. Mendum.

B. P. 3600.48.

N. Y., Y C O 11-15957/

L. of C., B. 2053. S g 3 E 6.

—. The System of Nature; or, The Laws of the Moral and Physical World, by the baron d'Holbach, originally attributed to M. de Mirabaud with memoir by Charles Bradlaugh. Reprinted verbatim from the best edition. London. Published by E. Truelove, 256 High Holborn, 1884. In 8vo, pp. xi + 520.

B. M. 8467 a a 33.

1772. Le Bon-sens ou idées naturelles opposées aux idées surnaturelles. Detexit quo doloso vaticinandi furore Sacerdotes mysteria, illis saepe ignota, audacter publicant—Petronii Satyricon. Londres (Amsterdam) 1772, 8vo, pp. xii - 515.

U. T. S. 321 H. 7236.

—. Ibid. Le Bon-sens du curé J. Meslier d'Etrépigny. Rome(Paris), 1791, 8vo.

—. Ibid. Another edition, 1772, 8vo, pp. x-250.

—. Ibid. Londres (Amsterdam), 1774, 16mo, pp. xii-302.

U. T. S. 321 H. 7236.

—. Ibid. Le Bon-sens du curé Meslier d'Etrépigny. Rome(Paris), 1791, 8vo.

—. Ibid. Nouvelle édition, suivi du Testament du curé

Meslier. Paris, Bouqueton, l'an I de la République. (1792, 2 vols., 12mo.)

—. Ibid. Le Bon-sens du curé J. Meslier suivi de son Testament. Paris, 1802, 8vo, pp. 380.
C. U. 843 M 56 D 1.

—. Ibid. Paris, Palais des Thermes de Julien, 1802 (1822), 12mo.

—. Ibid. Paris, Guillaumin, 1830, 12mo.

—. Ibid. Paris, Guillaumin, 1831, 12mo.

—. Common Sense, H. D. Robinson, New York, circa 1833.

—. Le Bon-sens du curé J. Meslier, etc. Paris, Bacquenois, 1833, 12mo.

—. Ibid. Paris, Guillaumin, 1834, 12mo.

—. Ibid. Nancy, Haener, 1834, 12mo.

—. Der gesunde Menschenverstand. Baltimore, 1857.

—. Ibid. Baltimore, 1859 (second edition), H. U.

—. Ibid Tr. into German by Miss Anna Knoop. circa 1878.

—. Ibid., under title, Superstition in all ages; by Jean Meslier... who left to the world the following pages entitled *Common Sense*. Translated from the French original by Miss Anna Knoop, New York, 1878.
C. U. L. 211 M.

—. Ibid. New York, Peter Eckler, 1890, pp. vi-339. U. T. S.

—. Le Bon-sens du curé J. Meslier, Paris, Palais des Thermes de Julien, 1802. (Garnier Frères, 1905. H. U.

—. Superstition in all ages, etc. Translated from the French original by Miss Anna Knoop; arranged for publication in its present form and manner with new title-page and preface by Dr. L. W. deLaurence. Same to now serve as "text-book" number five for "the congress of ancient, divine, mental and Christian masters," Chicago, Ill., DeLaurence, Scott & Co., 1910, pp. xx-17-339. L. of C. 1910, A 26880. L. W. de Laurence.

1772. De la nature humaine, ou Exposition des facultés, des actions et des passions de l'âme, et de leurs causes, déduites d'après des principes philosophiques qui ne sont communément ni reçus ni connus. Par Thomas Hobbes; Ouvrage traduit de l'Anglois. Londres (Amsterdam), MDCCLXXII. (8vo, pp. iv + 171.)

B. M. 8403 c c 15.

(Bookmark of Richard Chase Sidney.)

—. Ibid. Oeuvres philosophiques et politiques de Thomas Hobbes. 1787. (2 vols., 8vo.) (Tr. by Sorbière and Holbach.)

B. M. 528 2223.

1773. Recherches sur les Miracles. Par l'auteur de l'Examen des Apologistes de la Religion Chrétienne. A Genus attonitum. Ovid. Metam. Londres, MDCCLXXIII. (8vo. pp. 172.) B. M. 4015 de 44.

1773. La politique naturelle, ou, Discours sur les vrais principes du Governement. Par un ancien Magistrat. Vis consili expers mole ruit suâ. —Horat., Ode IV, lib. III, vers. 65 Londres (Amsterdam), MDCCLXXIII. (2 vols. in 8vo. pp. vii + 232 + 280.)

B. M. 521 h. 8.

U. S. 269 E. H. 723 (ex libris Baron Carl de Vinck, Ministre de Belgique).

C. U. 320 H. 691.

(Ascribed also to C. G. Lamoignon de Malesherbes.)

—. Ibid.Londres, 1774. (2 vols, in 8vo.)

—. La Politica Naturale: discorsi sui veri principi di governo. Traduzione di Luigi Salvadori. Mantova, Balbiani e Donelli, '78-80. (2 vols., 16 (L. 5).)

1773. Système Social, ou principes naturels de la moral et de la politique, avec un examen de l'influence du governement sur les moeurs.

Discenda virtus est, ars est bonum fieri; erras si

existimas vitia nobiscum nasci; supervenerunt in gesta sunt. —Seneca, Epis. 124. Londres, MDCCLXXIII. (8vo, pp. 218 + 174 + 166, in three parts.)

B. N., R 20275.76 E 1919.

C. U. 320. H. 69.

N. Y. SC.

—. Ibid. Par l'auteur du Système de la Nature, Londres, 1774. (3 vols., 8vo, pp. 208 + 174 + 167.)

B. M. 8403.h 23.

—. Ibid. A Paris, Servière, 1795. (2 vols., 8vo, pp. 472 + 403.)

B. M. 8404 dc. 25 (ex libris J. Gomez de la Cortina et amicorum. Fallitur hora legendo).

—. Ibid....par le baron d'Holbach. Paris, Niogret, 1882. (2 vols, 8vo.)

C. U. 320. H. 690.

1774. Agriculture réduit à ses vrais principes par Jean Gottschalk Wallerius, Paris, Lacombe, 1774. (12mo.)

1776. Ethocratie ou le gouvernement fondé sur la morale.

Constituit bonos mores civitati princips. —Seneca, de Clementia, Lib. I.

A Amsterdam. Chez Marc Michel Rey. MDCCLXXVI. (8vo, pp. 10 + 293 + 2.)

C. U. 320. 1 H 69.

1776. Morale universelle, ou Les devoirs de l'homme fondés sur la nature.

Naturâ duce utendum est: hanc ratio observe, hanc consulit, idem est ergo beatè vivere et secundum naturam. —Seneca de Vita beata, Cap. VIII init.

A Amsterdam. Chez Marc-Michel Rey, MDCCLXXVI. (3 vols., 8vo, pp. 416 + 334 + 364.)

B. N., R 18596-7-8.

B. M. 231 h-3

—. Ibid. A Tours, Chez Letourmy le jeune et compagnie, A

Angers, De l'Imprimerie de Jahyer et Geslin. Imprimeurs-Libraries, rue Milton, 1792. (8vo.)

B. M. 527. K. 1-3.

H. U. Phil. 2648.50.

—. Ibid. Paris, Smith (Rey et Gravier), an 6, 1798. (3 vols., 8vo.)

—. Ibid. Par le baron d'Holbach. Paris, Masson et fils. Libraires, Rue de Tournon, No. 6, 1820. (3 vols., 8vo, pp. xxxii + 314 + 266 + 300.)

C. U. 170 H 2.

B. M. 8411 k 7.

—. Moral universal ódeberes del hombre, fundatos en su naturaleza Obra escrita en francès por el baron de Holbach y traducida al castellano por D. Manuel Diaz Moreno Zaragoza, 1838, imp. de M. Heras. (3 vols., 8vo.)

—. La moral universel por el baron de Holbach. Madrid, 1840, imp. y lib. del Establecimiento Central. (2 vols. in 4to.)

—. Ibid. Translated into German by Johann Umminger. Leipzig, 1898.

1790. Elements de la morale universelle, ou catechisme de la nature. Par feu M., le Baron d'Holbach des académies de Pétersbourg de Manheim et de Berlin.

Numquam aliud natura aliud sapientia dicit.—Juvenal.

A Paris. Chez G. de Bure. Rue Serpente, No. 6, MDCCXC. (24vo, pp. vi + 208.)

B. M. 528. a. 27.

B. P., G. 3537.14.

—. Elementos de la moral universel, ó catecismo de la naturaleza, por el baron de Holbach. Madrid, 1820, imp. que fué de Fuentenebro, lib de Sanchez en 8vo past.

—. Principios de moral, ó manuel de los deberes del hombre

fundados en la naturaleza. Obra póstuma de baron de Holbach. Traducida al espanol por D. L. M. G. adoptada en su mayor parte de la escuelas de primera educacion para instruccion de los ninos. Madrid, 1837, imp. de Ferrer y compania lib de J Sanz. (In 16mo.)

Bibliography. Part II.
General bibliography.

Allgemeine Deutsche Biographie.

Avézac-Lavigne, Diderot et la société du Baron d'Holbach. Paris, 1875.

Bachaumont, Mémoires secrètes. Paris, 1859.

Barbier, Dictionnaire des ouvrages anonymes et pseudonymes. Paris, 1822.

Barni, Histoire des idées morales et politiques en France au dix-huitième siècle. Paris, 1865.

Barruel, Mémoire pour servir à l'histoire de Jacobinisme. Hamburg, 1798.

Lettres helviennes. Hamburg, 1798-1799.

Bartholmess, Histoire philosophique de l'Académie de Prusse. Paris, 1851.

Bergier, Apologie de la Religion Chrétienne contre l'auteur du *Christianisme dévoilé*. Paris, 1769.

Examen du matérialisme, ou Réfutation du *Système de la Nature*. Paris, 1771.

Bibliothèque Nationale, Pièces originales. 1529 d'Holbach.

Manuscrits Français, 15224, 22149 (Col. Anisson).

Boiteau, Mémoires de Mme. d'Epinay. Paris.

British Museum Manuscript Index, 1876-1881. Mss. Folios 30867-69, 70, 71.

Brougham, A Discourse of Natural Theology. London, 1835.

Brunel, Les philosophes et l'Académie Française. Paris.

Brunet, Manuel du Librairie. Paris, 1865.

Bucherberger, Kirche-Lexikon.

Burton, Life and Correspondence of David Hume. Edinburgh, 1846.

Letters of Prominent Persons addressed to David Hume. Edinburgh and London, 1849.

Buzonnière, Observations sur un ouvrage intitulé le *Système de la Nature*. Paris, 1776.

Camuset, Principes contre l'incrédulité, à l'occasion du *Système de la Nature*. Paris, 1771.

Carlile, The Deist. London, 1819.

Carlyle, Rev. Dr. Alexander, Autobiography, Ed. Burton. London, 1861.

Castillon, Observations sur un livre intitulé, *Système de la Nature*. Berlin, 1771.

Catalogue des manuscrits français dans les bibliothèques départementales.

Chaudon, Dictionnaire anti-philosophique etc. Avignon, 1767.

Claudon, Le Baron d'Holbach. Paris, 1835.

Collignon, Diderot. Paris, 1907.

Critica, 1903-1904

Damiron, Mémoires pour servir à l'histoire de la philosophie au 18me siècle. Paris, 1858.

Etudes sur la philosophie de d'Holbach. Mémoires de l'Académie des sciences morales et politiques, Vol. IV du Compte rendu des Séances.

Debure, Catalogue des livres de la bibliothèque du feu M. le baron d'Holbach. Paris, 1789.

Delisle de Sales, Philosophie de la Nature. Paris, 1770.

Mémoire en faveur de Dieu. Paris, 1802.

Delvaille, Essai sur l'histoire de l'idée de progrès. Paris, 1910.

Diderot, Oeuvres, ed Brière. Paris, 1822.

Mémoires, correspondance, et ouvrages inédits de Diderot. Paris, 1830.

Oeuvres complètes de Diderot, ed. Assézat et Tourneux. Paris, 1877.

Douarche, Les tribunaux civils de Paris pendant la Révolution. Paris, 1905-1907.

Dupont de Nemours, Philosophie de l'univers. Paris, l'An IV (1796).

Duprat, Les Encyclopédists. Paris, 1865.

Duvoisin, L'Autorité des livres du Nouveau Testament contre les incrédules. Paris, 1775.

L'Autorité des livres de Moïse, etc. Paris, 1778.

Eclaircissements relatifs à la publication des *Confessions* de Rousseau, avec des réflexions sur les apologies de MM. Cerutti et d'Holbach etc. Paris, 1789.

Encyclopédie des sciences religieuses.

Epinay, Mme. d' Mémoires et correspondance. Paris, 1818.

Fabre, Les Pères de la Révolution. De Bayle à Condorcet. Paris, 1910.

Fabry d'Autrey, Antiquité justifiée etc. Paris, 1766.

Fangouse, La religion prouvée aux incrédules, etc. Paris, 1780.

Ferraz, Histoire de la philosophie pendant la Révolution. Paris, 1889.

Histoire de la philosophie en France au 19me siecle. Paris, 1882.

Fitzmaurice, Life of William, Earl of Shelburne. London, 1875.

Fortnightly Review, Vol. XXVIII, 1877.

Frederick II, King of Prussia, Examen critique du livre intitulé *Système de la Nature*. Berlin, 1770.

Fréret, Lettre de Thrasybule à Leucippe.

Funck, Les sophistes français et la révolution européenne. Paris, 1905.

Galiani, Lettres, ed. E. Asse. Paris.

Correspondance, ed. Perey et Maugras. Paris, 1910.

Garrick. Private Correspondence. London, 1833.

Gasté, Diderot et le curé de Montchauvet, etc. Paris, 1898.

Garat, Mémoires historiques sur le 18me siècle. Paris, 1821.

Gazette de France, Aug. 10, 1754. June 1, 1781.

Genlis, Mme de, Les dîners du Baron d'Holbach, etc. Paris, 1822.

Gibbon, Autobiography, ed. Murray. London, 1897.

Private Letters, 1753-1794, ed Prothero. London, 1897.

Grande Encyclopédie.

Grimm, Correspondance littéraire et critique. Paris, 1878.

Nouveaux mémoires secrets et inédits, etc. Paris, 1834.

Hammard, Mme. de Genlis. New York, 1913.

Hancock, The French Revolution and the English Poets. New York, 1899.

Hedgcock, David Garrick et ses amis français. Paris, 1911.

Helvetius, Le vrai sens du *Système de la Nature*. Paris, 1774.

Herzog, Real-Encyklopedie.

Hibbert, A Short Sketch of the Life and the Writings of Baron d'Holbach. London, 1834.

Holland, Réflexions philosophiques sur la *Système de la Nature*. Paris, 1822.

Hume, Private Correspondence, etc. London, 1820.

L'Impie démasqué, etc. London, 1773.

Independent Whig. London, 1720.

Jal, Dictionnaire critique de biographie et d'histoire. Paris, 1867.

Journal de lecture, Vol. I, 1775.

Journal de Paris, 1789.

Laharpe, Cours de littérature. Paris, 1821.
Philosophie du 18me siècle. Paris, 1818.
Lagrange, Oeuvres complètes de Senèque. Paris, 1778.
Landry, Beccaria, Scritte e lettre inediti. 1910.
Lange, History of Materialism. Boston, 1877.
Lanson, Manuel bibliographique de la littérature française moderne 1500-1900. Paris, 1911.
Lenel, Un homme de lettres au 18me siècle, Marmontel. Paris, 1902.
Lerminier, De l'influence de la philosophie au 18 siècle. Paris, 1833.
Lévy-Bruhle, History of Modern Philosophy in France. Chicago, 1899.
Lowell, The Eve of the French Revolution. Boston, 1892.
Magasin encyclopédique. Mai, 1805.
Mangold, von, Unumstossliche Widerlegung des Materialismus gegen den Verfasser des Systèms der Natur. Augsburg, 1803.
Maréchal, Dictionnaire des athées (Paris). An. VIII (1800).
Marmontel, Mémoires, ed. Tourneur. Paris, 1891.
Martin, Histoire de France, 1748-1789. 4th Ed.
Michaud, Biographie universelle.
Morellet, Mémoires. Paris, 1821.
Lettres à Lord Shelburne. Paris, 1898.
Mornet, Les sciences de la nature au 18me siècle. Paris, 1911.
Myers, Konversations-Lexikon.
Naigeon, Mémoires historiques et philosophiques sur la vie et les ouvrages de Denis Diderot. Paris, 1821.
Nouvelle Revue, June, July, 1912.
Paulian, La religion prouvée aux incrédules, etc. Paris, 1780.
Paulian, Le véritable système de la nature. Paris, 1788.
Payrard, De la nature et de ses lois. Paris, 1773.

Perey et Maugras, Dernières années de Mme. d'Epinay. Paris, 1883.

Picavet, Les Idéologues. Paris, 1891.

Plechanow, Beiträge zur Geschichte des Materialismus. Stuttgart, 1896.

Quérard, La France littéraire. Paris, 1833.

Supercheries littéraires dévoilées. Paris, 1870.

Littérature française contemporaine (Continuation).

Rabbe, Biographie.

Répertoire de la Gazette de France.

Revue Bleue, June, 1912.

Revue de l'histoire littéraire de la France, Jan.-June, 1912.

Revue de synthèse historique, 1903, Vol. I.

Revue des Cours et Conférences, 1908-1910.

Revue des deux mondes, Apr., 1886; June, 1912.

Revue encyclopédique, Vol. XVI.

Rey, Rousseau. Paris, 1909.

Rietstap, Armorial général. Gonda, 1884.

Robinet, Le personnel municipale de Paris pendant la Révolution. Paris, 1890.

Rochfort, L'Esprit révolutionnaire avant la Révolution. Paris, 1878.

Romilly, Sir S., Memoirs. London, 1840.

Rosenkrantz, Diderot's Leben und Werke. Leipzig, 1864.

Rousseau, Oeuvres complètes. Paris, 1793.

Roustan, Les philosophes et la société française au 18me siècle. Paris, 1906.

St.-Beuve, Portraits littéraires. Paris, 1878.

Causeries de lundi. Paris, 1882.

St.-Martin, Des erreurs et de la vérité. Edinburgh, 1775.

Soury, Bréviaire de l'histoire de matérialisme. Paris, 1881.

Stupuy, Chez Diderot, comédie en deux actes, en vers. Paris, 1868.

Tallentyre, The Friends of Voltaire. London, 1906.

Villemain, Cours de littérature française. Paris, 1859.

Voltaire, Oeuvres complètes, ed. Beuchot. Paris, 1829-40.

Oeuvres complètes, ed. Garnier. Paris, 1880.

Walpole, H., Letters, ed, Toynbee. London, 1912.

Weiland, Oberon, tr. Holbach fils. Paris, 1825.

Wetzer & Welte, Kirchen-lexikon.

Wilkes, Correspondence with his Friends. London, 1805.

Letters from the year 1774 to 1796, addressed to his daughter. London, 1805.

Wright, A History of French Literature. London, 1912.

Vita

Max Pearson Cushing, born in Bangor, Maine, October 27, 1886; Bangor High School, 1905; A.B. Bowdown College, 1909. Instructor in English, Robert College, Constantinople, 1909-1911; Graduate Student in History, Columbia University, 1911-1913; A.M. Columbia, 1912, Instructor in History, Reed College, Portland, Oregon, 1913.

Also from Benediction Classsics...

Hardback, 2011, 980 pages, ISBN: 9781849023122

John Stuart Mill's 'System of Logic, Ratiocinative and Inductive' was a ground-breaking work of philosophy, first published in 1843. Mill espoused the empiricist view of political and social philosophy, and formulated the five principles of inductive reasoning that are known as Mill's Methods. The two original volumes of the seventh edition have here been brought together into a single book, which has been carefully edited to be accurate and readable.

www.ingramcontent.com/pod-product-compliance
Lightning Source LLC
Chambersburg PA
CBHW022115280326
41933CB00007B/394